professional
perspectives

D1512683

Dealing with Difficulties

Solutions, strategies and suggestions for successful teaching

Lindsay Clandfield
Luke Prodromou

DELTA
PUBLISHING

Published by
DELTA PUBLISHING
Quince Cottage
Hoe Lane
Peaslake
Surrey GU5 9SW
England

© Delta Publishing 2007

First published 2007

ISBN 978-1-905085-00-2

Edited by Tanya Whatling
Designed by Christine Cox
Illustrations by Phillip Burrows
Project managed by Chris Hartley
Printed by Halstan & Co., Amersham,
Bucks, England

Acknowledgements

Lindsay

I would like to thank all the classes I've had that made
my life difficult as a teacher (you know who you are!).
Without them I would never have thought of a book like
this.

I would also like to thank all those people around the
world who volunteer their time to set up ELT conferences.
I met Luke Prodromou at such a conference in Granada,
Spain in 2001. The idea of working together on this
project was born there. Conferences are great places to
meet people and make things happen.

I used to wonder why authors thanked their editors in
the acknowledgements. Now I know. Thank you Mike
Burghall for keeping us going and helping us overcome
any difficulties we had writing this book.

Thanks also to Joaquín Gerardo for his motivating talks
on dealing with mixed-ability classes which came just
at the right time.

Finally, to my wife, Sofia: merci pour tout.

This book is for my sons, Lucas and Marcos.

Luke

My thanks go to:

Lindsay Clandfield for helping me grow.

Mike Burghall for his systematic and creative editing.

All the colleagues on whose shoulders we have stood
in order to write this book; of these, Mario Rinvolucri
deserves special thanks for being a constant source of
inspiration over so many years

I dedicate the book to my wife, Kiveli, and children:
Michael, Antony and Rosa.

Personal Prefaces

Lindsay Clandfield

The activist and teacher James Baldwin once said that 'the price one pays for pursuing any profession or calling is an intimate knowledge of its ugly side'. I was initially trained in communicative methodology and practised with a small group of motivated native-speaker trainee teachers. When I first came to ELT, I had grand and noble ideas about what I would do with my classes. I was in for a rude awakening.

My first real job was at a university in Mexico. Like many teachers there, I took another job in a high school to supplement my income. All of a sudden, many of the techniques I had learned didn't work – I had classes of between twenty-seven and forty-five students (instead of eight), and little or no equipment. I couldn't move the furniture easily in the room. My students didn't bring their coursebooks to class, never did any homework and spent a lot of their time chatting to each other in Spanish. Teaching was a real struggle.

Very many teachers suffer these problems in silence, or simply complain about them in the staffroom, and I was no exception. I came across similar difficulties in classrooms in Spain, the UK, Canada and the Czech Republic.

It wasn't until I started looking for help that things began to get better.

- I was lucky to meet other, more experienced, teachers who gave me tips and advice.
- I started to read around the subject and experiment with different ways of tackling difficulties.
- I began to realise that other teachers had many of the same problems and this helped reduce the feeling of guilt that I had about my classes.

Dealing with Difficulties is a product of my own difficult teaching experiences. And it is a product of all the inspiring teachers I have observed putting into successful practice activities such as the ones here.

Teaching a well-behaved and motivated class is one of the best jobs in the world. With the help of many of the techniques and activities in this book, I have succeeded in working with motivated and well-behaved classes.

And I can still say that my initial ideas and ideals about teaching weren't entirely wrong after all.

Luke Prodromou

The origins of this book, for me, can be traced back to one of the first classes I ever taught, in 1973, when my only qualification to teach English was that I had a degree in English literature and a passion for Shakespeare. I soon realised that *Hamlet* was not much use to me when teaching the verb 'to be' to truculent teenagers. The Prince of Denmark had, moreover, little to say about discipline problems in large mixed-level classes, overcrowded with adolescents and their unruly hormones. Some of them, male **and** female, simply refused to pay me any attention. Indeed, they actually seemed to get pleasure out of ignoring me and chatting happily amongst themselves. I felt excluded by their laughter and the more I tried to control them, the louder my voice got and the deeper I sank into the swamp of indiscipline.

I had discovered that teaching English was more than just teaching grammar and vocabulary: it was also about dealing with difficulties such as noisy, unmotivated youngsters and the huge variation in ability and learning styles in the same class. Getting students' attention and keeping it seemed to be the be-all and end-all of teaching.

My main strategy in dealing with these difficulties was to 'kick out' the ringleaders, who would sometimes refuse to leave the room and even challenged my authority head-on. The 'weak' learners were simply penalised with a low grade in the frequent tests I had to administer. Indeed, it was mostly at examination times that my class tended to calm down somewhat.

I had accidentally bumped into my first 'discipline-friendly' technique: testing, which was bad for teaching but good for discipline.

However, I never lost hope in our capacity to deal with difficulties because I saw how the same unruly bunch of kids could become, as if by magic, almost angelic in the hands of a teacher with good rapport, positive attitudes and strong presence. Yet these qualities are not easy to teach.

Dealing with Difficulties is an attempt to translate some of that magic into tips, techniques and a practical methodology. The suggestions you will find here are, potentially, steps for overcoming the difficulties that get in the way of enjoyable teaching and learning.

Contents

Introduction

This book is for teachers of all levels and all ages in both the private and the public sector, in language contexts where resources are abundant and where resources are scarce. However fortunate our teaching situation may be, none of us is free from at least some of the difficulties addressed here.

This book is for teachers like the one who wrote a letter to one of the authors following a workshop on learner-centred methodology and who included a set of rules for her 'new revolutionary method for teaching English to little monsters'. Her rules were more or less as follows:

- There is only one teacher in class and not only does she know what she's doing, but she is always right.
- When the teacher speaks, the little devils – or so-called 'learners' – will be quiet and pay attention. They cannot interrupt.
- Silence will be observed at all times. If they want to practise speaking, they can do it at home, in their own time.
- Pupils will not do what they think, but what they are told.

The language used – *devils, monsters* – reflects the profound alienation and sense of despair this teacher has reached. This book is a gesture of solidarity and an attempt to offer constructive solutions to the problems she identifies.

We have often felt that innovative methodologies – communicative, task-based and humanistic – fall, and often fail, on the stony ground of classrooms where both learners and teachers lack motivation. This book is a response to teachers who feel like giving up on their students, often quite understandably, for the sake of their own peace of mind. Teaching classes of unruly children or adolescents, and even classes of unmotivated adults, can be a stressful, demoralising business. Good teaching practice cannot flourish in such circumstances.

Identifying the Difficulties

In teaching, in training and especially in observing teachers at work in all sectors, we have identified the following as the most common difficulties faced by teachers:

- mixed levels
- large classes
- getting students' attention
- keeping students' attention
- getting students to do homework
- getting lessons off to a good start
- discipline
- teacher burn-out
- dominance of testing over teaching
- encouraging independent learning
- inability or unwillingness to adapt textbooks
- ending lessons smoothly.

We have organised these topics into the different chapters in the book and we attempt to deal with them by offering solutions and strategies for a more successful classroom.

Dealing with the Difficulties

Oddly enough, the question of discipline and mixed-level classes is not one of the most frequent at teachers' conferences and seminars. We hear more about the latest research into language learning and cutting-edge methodologies than the bread-and-butter issues of controlling a class. There are dozens of books on motivation, communicative interaction, games in the classroom, task-based learning, and almost any subject related to teaching English, but books on what to do when students make life difficult for the teacher are few and far between. With this book we have tried to break the near-silence surrounding discipline and other 'difficulties'.

The approach taken is, first, to examine the problem in a positive light and to try to see the opportunities for learning in what we often assume is simply a threat or an obstacle. The second stage is to eliminate the negative aspect of the difficulty by suggesting constructive solutions.

1 Large Classes and Classroom Management

This chapter focuses on aspects of managing large classes but will offer useful insights and tips into working with smaller groups, too. We are often struck by the fact that a good knowledge of language or methodology is not necessarily enough to make one a successful teacher. The sense of time and pace, the use of space and the ability to energise a group of people brought together on a random basis are essential, if elusive, skills in the classroom. These skills are vital when teaching both large and small classes.

2 Discipline Problems

This chapter looks at the many different kinds of indiscipline in the classroom. We need to explore the root causes of some of the many ways of disrupting a class before we can suggest a range of tips and activities for beginning to tackle this most intractable of all classroom problems.

3 Mixed-level Classes

This chapter argues that all classes are 'mixed ability' – that is, they all include diversity. An important first step is to see this diversity in a positive light and to make the most of the opportunities it offers. The techniques described in this chapter are organised in such a way as to help you see and structure your classes differently.

4 Homework

This chapter looks at strategies on how to maximise the effectiveness of homework in a variety of ways. Homework is a neglected resource, both outside and inside the classroom. This chapter looks at the challenge of homework on two levels: getting students to do it in the first place and, secondly, persuading students of the value of homework.

5 Teaching Exam Classes

The distinction between a 'testing' and a 'teaching' approach to learning is at the heart of the difficulties of teaching exam classes. On the one hand, it is the easiest thing in the world for the teacher to slip into the role of 'examiner' – one who has the right answers and simply seeks to check whether the students know the right answers – but this is usually done at the cost of sacrificing the best qualities we have as teachers. This chapter offers ways of maintaining the balance between testing and teaching.

6 Professional Development

The difficulties we have outlined above are not few, and, combined, they can really wear a teacher down. There are, however, ways to fight this. Whether it is with their colleagues, with the whole school or in the context of the wider educational world, or through reading ELT magazines, journals or many of the fascinating books written about every aspect of language teaching, teachers stand a much better chance of not burning out if they are continually developing professionally.

Dealing with Diversity

There's no success like failure and failure's no success at all. Bob Dylan

Many words related to the subject of this book are loaded with negative attitudes towards teaching and the learner; and they tend to be words beginning with 'd': *attention deficit, disorder, demotivation, discipline.* Indeed 'd' is usually a fail grade in tests! We can sum these attitudes up as the 'difficulties' many teachers face in dealing with group dynamics rather than any difficulty with the English language as such.

It is an underlying assumption in this book that difficulties can not only be dealt with but transformed into opportunities for further learning. This is by no means an easy task but it is the only one that opens the way to more pleasant and productive teaching and learning. The key is to see *diversity* (another 'd' word!) as a positive feature in the classroom. It is not an obstacle but a potential resource that can make learning richer by drawing on what the students bring to class and thus raising their self-esteem and their respect for each other.

It is the process of transforming failure into success.

Dealing with Difficulties

Dealing with Difficulties

So exactly how is the book organised?

The **Introductions** to the various chapters set the scene – and we hope the scene is not a bleak one if we draw on our potential for development, which often means awareness of the nature of the problem and the options available to us. This is where 'theory' or broad methodological issues come in. The Introductions include things that you might like to ask yourself or think about to promote your own development and awareness of the topic under discussion.

The **Tips and Techniques** sections are packed with practical advice where 'recipes' cannot apply. They are ideas for how you can come up with appropriate responses to your own problems in class. They bring us closer to the solution by suggesting strategies or a way out of the difficulty.

The **Activities** are ones we and other teachers have found helpful in getting through a difficult class. They are, on one level, 'recipes' but they are not so much 'things-to-do-on-a-rainy-Friday-afternoon' as techniques that can be adapted and actually change ways of teaching They differ from recipes in that we hope you can adapt them and arrive at your own practical solutions to your own problems. The Activities are, in other words, generative, rather than 'one-offs'.

All the Activities follow a set of headings to allow you to see at a glance what is involved.

Level
The majority of the activities in this book are suitable for any level, including, and especially, mixed-level classes. Some activities are marked 'From elementary onwards' or 'From intermediate onwards' which means that they can be perfectly adapted for higher levels, but are not suitable for levels lower than the one specified.

Aim
This tells you what a particular activity is about, in terms of helping to provide strategies for successful teaching.

Duration
This tells you how long an activity lasts. The duration times are estimates based on our own experience and watching others teach. Don't feel restricted by the number of minutes indicated!

Materials
This tells you what you need for the activity. Most activities in this book require no materials at all, barring the teacher, the students and something to write on. When this is not the case, it is indicated here.

Language / Skills
This tells you what language you may expect from the activity (when applicable) and what skills (listening, reading, speaking, writing) are being practised.

Preparation
This tells you what you need to prepare in advance. We know that you already have lots to do, so we have tried to make the vast majority of the activities require little or no preparation at all.

Procedure
This gives step-by-step instructions on what to do in class to ensure a successful outcome of the activity.

1

Large Classes and Classroom Management

*'In my initial teacher training, we never had more than fifteen students.
I am now teaching classes of over thirty. It's a whole different story.'*

Many of us are faced daily with large classes. In fact, some teachers start work with large classes without any prior teaching practice at all. Speaking in public is difficult for many people, and the bigger the public, the more difficult it can seem.

This chapter is about dealing with a large class. A 'large class' is a subjective term. For some, it is eighteen or nineteen students. For some, it is forty and for others, a large class is 100 to 200 students. Most of the activities we recommend here can be used effectively with classes of up to fifty people.

But dealing with a large group of people is only one part of the equation. There are other fundamental issues of classroom management that, if ignored, can cause us problems even in the smallest, most manageable of classes. This chapter also deals with several aspects of classroom management that are useful for any size of class, including those big ones.

1.1 Managing Big Numbers

'There's a real problem in keeping control with so many students. I have to shout all the time.'

The first section of this chapter provides activities and ideas relating to classroom control and adapting activities. One of the greatest challenges for any teacher faced with a large class is the sense of not feeling in control. There are a number of factors that can contribute to this sense of being lost. It may be on that particular day the class is distracted by something else and there is little you can do about it. It may be that environmental factors (excessive heat or cold in the classroom) make it difficult for anyone to concentrate for any period of time. These are factors that are beyond one's control. But the truth is that many factors affecting classroom control are in the teacher's hands. Here is a short list:

- knowing, and using, students' names
- using the space to your advantage
- checking and cross-checking
- making eye contact
- using the board effectively
- being organised and prepared
- having routines.

Another way of putting this is that if you do **not** do the above there is a greater likelihood that you will lose control – or, at least, the feeling of control.

1.2 Starting Right

'I don't know how to start a class. They just don't seem interested.'

The second section deals with the beginning of classes. Starting a class is a crucial phase of any lesson. Like a good book or film, the first few minutes should engage your attention so you follow the main part of the story with greater interest and involvement.

Many of the activities described here are also designed to develop and strengthen rapport in class. Rapport is the positive relationships we try to build and without which little can happen. How you start the lesson sets the tone for what will follow and establishes the kind of relationships you wish to create amongst your students.

1.3 Handling Latecomers

'There are always two or three students who come in five or ten minutes late. It disrupts my class and really bothers me.'

The tips and techniques in section three all address the issue of latecomers. One common 'difficulty' in every class is the fact that people have rhythms of their own: some arrive on time, others arrive late. Whatever we do, students will tend to turn up in class at slightly different times and this often threatens the cohesion of the group and the rhythm of the lesson. Latecomers disrupt the class and distract the teacher who might be in mid-explanation, often making noise when they ask a partner what they have missed! The infamous latecomers are a headache and a problem for many of us.

You may be working in a school environment which already has rules and procedures for latecomers. But many teachers are in a situation where they have to make or break the rules themselves and they find it difficult to deal with people who come in those five, ten or fifteen minutes late. Something **can** be done, but what? There are three possible options for the teacher to deal with this problem:

- ignore it and hope it goes away
- devise forfeits to 'punish' the latecomer (a 'stick' approach)
- devise incentives to 'reward' those who come on time (a 'carrot' approach).

However, the challenge really lies in not only 'dealing with' the problem (often reactively) but, rather, in taking advantage of it proactively to make learning more interesting and effective.

1.4 Engaging Students with the Material

'When I tell students to take out their books, they look so bored. Even before they see what's in the book.'

Section four explores ways of engaging a class with the theme of the lesson while their books are still closed. If you are working with a coursebook, most lessons will be built around a theme (food, family, love, environment, etc.). Instead of beginning the lesson with the instruction *Open your books on page …*, try to engage the students' interest **before** they open their books.

1.5 Moving Students Around

'My students always want to work together in cliques. I often feel like a dictator when I split them up.'

The activities in section five show you how to integrate this aspect of classroom management into the normal routine of teaching language and building rapport, even with large numbers. Rearranging the seating in a class may be necessary at the beginning or at any point during the lesson itself. The ability to get students to move without dragging their heels, causing an uproar or simply refusing, is important and may make or break a lesson. Furthermore, moving students and setting up pairs and groups can itself be an opportunity for language practice.

1.6 Drilling

'I feel bad that my classes aren't more communicative, but with so many students it's just not possible.'

The activities in the sixth section are a small selection of drills and controlled activities that work particularly well with large groups of students.

In big mixed-level classes, students often lack the confidence to perform in a foreign language in front of the whole class. 'Solo performances', riddled with errors of grammar, vocabulary and pronunciation, are not everyone's cup of tea. So before we consider the open-ended skill of 'speaking', we might usefully look at an activity that seems more accessible to teachers of big classes, as well as to their students. However, in recent years 'drilling' has had a mixed press. Many teachers view drills as belonging to an outdated methodology (which offered little else). They are also seen as being not very communicative, meaningless and mindless. But there is a certain pleasure in repetition and chants which is magnified in larger numbers. There is also solid research evidence that repetition in general is an important dimension of how we learn a language. Controlled activities, whether drill-like or repetition-rich, can also instil a sense of confidence in someone faced with an intimidating grammatical structure or speaking activity. The choral element provides a screen behind which 'quieter' students can hide and discreetly build up their confidence. Controlled practice can take the form of choral drills, as described above, but the downside of these is often that they are mechanical, dull and boring. The alternate use of chants and rhymes adds an element of fun and creativity to controlled practice.

1.7 Speaking

'All the good communicative activities only work with small groups, but I have over thirty people in my class.'

The seventh section of this chapter includes activities to get your students communicating orally in large classes. In language teaching, speaking is often considered the holy chalice. For many teachers of large classes, the idea of a speaking activity immediately brings to mind images of mayhem and chaos. Indeed, this will often be true if speaking activities are not carefully set up and students

don't know what to do. Whereas drills are more accuracy-based, the speaking activities in this section are fluency-based, which means that you may want to save the correction of any spoken errors until after the activity is finished, if you correct at all.

1.8 Finishing Right

'I often find I run out of time at the end of the class, and we'll sometimes finish mid-activity.'

The final section suggests activities to round off a class on a positive note. One of the elements of a successful class is how it finishes. Added to which, controlling the timing and fragmentation of large classes (e.g. during groupwork) is more difficult. Whether you build the class up to a grand finale or bring it to a soft landing is a matter of choice, as long as you convey clearly that the class is finished. Ending on a good note will, hopefully, make your students more enthusiastic about coming back the next time.

Many coursebook materials are not written specifically with a class of more than twenty in mind. However, a large number of students can in fact enhance some of these activities. And in large classes there is a much richer variety of backgrounds, personal histories, world views and experiences than in a small class of eight people, for example.

In a large class there seem to be so many things that are hard to get right and yet, as we have seen, we can identify some basic things that we can do to make things work better. Basic classroom management is fundamental. There is little point in trying to do something a little different if half of the students don't understand because they can't hear you or if they aren't listening. Classroom management is all about how we handle time and space – classroom time and classroom space. It is also about how we manage people (the students and our relationship with them) and the objects in the room.

It is easy to forget how ever-present these factors are and how they affect the impact of what we do in class in so many subtle, elusive and yet potentially crucial ways. Let's look more closely, then, at managing time, space, people and objects so we can grab students' attention – and keep it!

The Attention-getter

Level	Any
Aim	To organise the class
Duration	10 minutes
Materials	None
Skills / Language	Understanding instructions; speaking practice

Preparation

Decide and prepare what your attention-getter signal is going to be (see box opposite, on page 13).

Procedure

1 Tell the class that because they are going to be speaking a lot in pairs and groups, there will often be a lot of noise. It is important for them to know what they have to do and when to stop. For this reason, there will be times when you will need all their attention. Explain that on these occasions you will show them a signal. When they see or hear the signal, they should stop what they are doing and look towards you. Show them the attention-getter signal and explain that for the next activity you are going to practise the signal with them.

2 Write the following on the board and indicate to the class to find their groups:

Work in groups of three or four maximum.

3 Let the students organise themselves into groups of three. When the noise level begins to rise, give the signal. Praise the class once they stop and look towards you.

4 Write the following on the board and signal to the class with your hands to begin talking:

Tell each other three <u>true</u> things about yourself and one lie.

5 Let the conversation continue until you are satisfied most students have completed the task. Give the signal and praise them again once they turn to pay attention to you.

6 Write on the board:

Guess which of the four facts you heard was a lie.

7 Repeat the same process again.

Follow-up

Use the attention-getter signal regularly in class.

NOTE: We recommend against using a shouted 'OK!' or 'Right!' as the signal. The students might not hear this over the other people talking, and repeatedly shouting and straining is bad for your voice.

Group Leaders

Level	Any
Aim	To organise the class
Duration	15 minutes
Materials	Pen and paper; envelopes
Skills / Language	Functional language for making requests; reading comprehension

Preparation

Make a copy of the Group Leader Task Sheet for every four or five students in the class and place in individual envelopes. This could be in the students' own language if they are very low-level (see box opposite, on page13).

Procedure

1 Tell the class you want them to organise themselves into groups of four or five. They do not need to move chairs or desks around for this (indeed, this may be impossible if furniture is screwed down). Allow them some time to decide who the groups are.

2 Write the following dialogue on the board:

    A: *Can I have it, please?*
    B: *Sure, here you go.*
    A: *Thanks.*

3 Practise this dialogue as a whole class, saying each line one at a time and asking them to repeat together.

4 Distribute one envelope (with the task sheet inside) to each group. Tell them to pass the envelope around the group, using the dialogue. Demonstrate with a student. Once they get the hang of it, encourage them to go faster.

5 Give the signal for everyone to stop (see The Attention-getter on page 13 opposite).

6 Tell the class that whoever is holding the envelope should open it and follow the instructions. They will be the group leaders.

7 Collect the names of the groups and group leaders.

Follow-up

Do this activity every week, every two weeks or whenever you want to change group leaders. Use the group leaders to do the following tasks:

- reporting back on group speaking tasks
- checking answers to exercises done by the group and reaching consensus before reporting back
- collecting written work and handing it in
- going through correct answers for exercises (you can prepare copies of the answer key for group leaders beforehand).

The Board Plan

Level	Any
Aim	To organise the class
Duration	3–5 minutes
Materials	None
Skills / Language	Reading

Preparation

Before class, write the main points of your lesson on the board (see The Board Plan opposite). Put the plan in the top left hand corner of the board. Research shows that this is where the eye is drawn to (think of where icons and menus tend to be on computer screens). Put the plan in the same place every day.

Procedure

1 At the beginning of class, show the class the points you have listed on the board. Briefly explain each one.

2 As the lesson progresses, cross out, erase or tick each point as you finish it.

Variation

Sometimes you may want to include a 'surprise' in your plan (a game, a test) and the effect could be ruined by writing it up and explaining it. In this case, merely write *Surprise* for that activity. As you go through the plan, add a little bit of suspense. For example: *After our reading activity, we have a little ... surprise. Now what could it be? Maybe a game, maybe a test. We'll see.*

NOTE: Going through the plan like this ahead of time can be immensely satisfying for students. Often you, the teacher, having planned the whole lesson, can see the learning outcomes and achievement of aims. But from the students' point of view the aims may not be so clear. They may be asking themselves why they were actually doing an activity. Going through the main points of the class and crossing them out as you go gives a sense of progress.

The Attention-getter Signals

- raising a hand in the air
- raising two hands in the air
- ringing a bell
- clicking the lights on and off
- holding up and waving some kind of distinctive object (a colourful feather or a flag)
- showing a blank transparency on the overhead projector
- moving to the back or to a specific part of the room and making a signal
- tapping lightly on the microphone, if you are using one, when it is turned on.

Group Leaders Task Sheet

Congratulations! You are the leader for your group. You are going to help the teacher and the other students.

- Write the names of the other students in your group on a piece of paper.
- Write your name at the top of the paper.
- Next to your name, write: *Group Leader*.
- When you have finished, give the paper to the teacher.

Thank you very much.

The Board Plan

<u>Thursday, January 15th</u>

Assign new group leaders
Vocabulary and Speaking – the family
Reading
Grammar: review – Present Simple
Pronunciation
Writing activity
Correct homework

Which Answers Are Different?

Level	Any
Aim	To encourage students to listen to each other
Duration	5 minutes
Materials	None
Skills / Language	Correcting written work or exercises

Procedure

1 After the students have finished an activity involving written answers (which have a right or wrong answer), ask them to compare answers with a partner and make a note of how many different answers they have.

2 Ask the pairs to check their answers with another pair and record how many different answers there are now.

3 Tell the students they now have two minutes to make any changes they wish to their answers.

4 Ask which answers are different now.

5 Go through and clarify those questions which had different answers.

NOTE: Once four students have compared their answers to a 'right / wrong' exercise, most of the errors have been peer-corrected. This saves you going through all the answers one by one. If there are still lots of differences in students' answers after peer consultation, then it is reasonable to believe that the exercise was too difficult in the first place.

Think, Pair, Share

Level	Any
Aim	To encourage interactive reading
Duration	10 minutes
Materials	Any reading comprehension text (or test) with questions
Skills / Language	Varied

Procedure

1 Write on the board or put up an overhead projector transparency that reads:

> **Think, Pair, Share**
> **Think** about your answer individually.
> **Pair** with a partner and discuss your answers.
> **Share** your answer (or your partner's answer) when called upon.

2 Ask the students to read the text you have chosen.

3 Ask them to close their books.

4 Ask the comprehension questions from the book, one by one. After the first question, draw the students' attention to the board or overhead transparency and ask them to follow the procedure.

5 Ask the second question, repeating the procedure as above. Continue with the rest of the questions.

Check, Cross-check

Level	Any
Aim	To maintain attention; to encourage students to listen to each other
Duration	2 minutes
Materials	None
Skills / Language	Varied

Procedure

1 After the students have finished a written activity or exercise, explain that you are going to go through the answers.

2 Call on a student to give you the answer to the first question.

3 When they give you an answer, regardless of whether or not it is correct, ask another student:
> *Do you agree?*
> *What did you answer, (John)?*

4 Repeat the process with the second question.

5 Keep moving around the classroom to extend your control over the whole class.

Variations

You can play the role of the slightly deaf teacher by saying:
Sorry, I didn't hear that. What did he / she say, (Sarah)?

Cross-checking can be used at various other points in the lesson as well:
- reporting back results of a discussion
- clarification of instructions
- explanations of grammar or vocabulary, etc.

Listen and Stand

Level	Any
Aim	To get the attention of a large class; introduce a 'difficult' listening or reading text kinaesthetically
Duration	10–15 minutes
Materials	An extract from a coursebook; pieces of paper
Skills / Language	Listening or reading

Preparation

Scan your listening or reading text for the words which you want to focus on. If possible, choose words which are repeated in the text. If you want to add your own repetition of a word, change the text by replacing the original words with the words you wish to focus on. See sample text below.

The words underlined will be the ones written on the students' slips of paper.

> The crowd behaved like animals. I suppose we hear that about twice a week nowadays. The crowd behaved like animals. Well, it just isn't true. Animals do not behave like that. Animals are not hooligans. They do not go around inflicting pain and destruction on their own kind. The behaviour of animals has more to do with the stability of their own species. They do not destroy their own kind in large numbers as human beings do. In fact, I'm amazed that animals have agreed to have anything to do with human beings at all.

Write the chosen words on pieces of paper.

Procedure

1 Give the slips of paper with the chosen words to different groups of students before they read or listen to the text. If your class is organised in straight rows, give each row of students the same word (you can do this by handing the slip of paper to the first student in the row, who passes it along until everyone has seen the word).

2 Tell the class you are going to read a text to them. Every time they hear the word which is written on their slip of paper (or any derivative of that word) they have to stand up and sit down again.

3 Read the text aloud (including any changes you have made in order to ensure repetition of the target words).

4 Ask the class to recall which words each group stood up to.

5 Ask them to tell you **exactly** what the text said.

6 The students read or listen to the original text and the lesson proceeds as 'normal'.

NOTE: This activity is based on an idea by Ken Wilson. It is an ideal activity for a large class.

- It always manages to raise a laugh.
- It gets the attention of a large class.
- It eases the students gently into what might be a difficult text.
- It gives them a sense of 'ownership' of the text: standing up when they hear 'their' word makes the text more familiar, friendlier. When they listen to or read the original text, they are driven forward by the knowledge that their words are buried in the text.

Entry Music

Level	Any
Aim	To build rapport and create an 'English classroom' space
Duration	2 minutes at the beginning of class
Materials	A recording of 'theme music' to begin the class; a CD / cassette player
Skills / Language	None

Preparation
Get to class five minutes before your students and cue up the music you would like the students to hear as they arrive, so you are not fiddling with the machine as the first ones enter.

Procedure
1 Set the mood for the English class by having music playing as students come in. Greet the students, but don't make a big thing of the music. It should be 'background music'.

2 Leave the music on as they get to their desks, take out their pens and books and get settled.

3 When you turn the music off it will provide a break, at which point it is easier to get everyone's attention and begin the class.

NOTE: You can have different music for different kinds of day. Here are some suggestions:
- a bouncy pop song for a sunny day (especially if it is the first sunny day in ages)
- a heavy piece of classical music (Beethoven or Wagner) for a test
- light classical music (Vivaldi or Bach) for a normal day
- topical songs for times of the year (e.g. Christmas, Halloween, Valentine's Day)
- music by a certain artist if that person has been in the news (e.g. if Coldplay has come to town and you know some of the students saw them, play Coldplay in the background).

Who's Here?

Level	Any
Aim	To take the class register
Duration	5 minutes (depending on how many students there are in your class)
Materials	None
Skills / Language	Listening and speaking; vocabulary review

Procedure
1 Choose a vocabulary area you would like the students to review. It should be quite a big category (e.g. food, drinks, clothes, sports, parts of the body, etc.).

2 Write the category on the board.

3 Tell the students that you are going to take the register. When you call out a student's name, they must answer with a word in English. It should be a word from the category you have written on the board.

Variations
Ask the students to answer with a word beginning with a certain letter.

Ask them to answer with a phrase that indicates how ready they are for the class. For example:
Present and feeling … good / ready / excited / happy / tired / bored / ill.

NOTE: Taking the register is one classroom routine that we have to deal with on a daily basis. It is also a routine that is ripe for breeding boredom and misbehaviour, especially with large numbers. The image of the teacher monotonously reading out students' names to sullen answers of 'present' is familiar to many. Once we are familiar with the class, we will often dispense with the roll call, filling out the attendance sheet at the end of the class as students are filing out. This is a shame, because with a little imagination, the mere calling out of students' names can be made into something more interesting.

Split Jokes

Level	From intermediate onwards
Aim	To get students' attention; to create a relaxed atmosphere
Duration	10 minutes
Materials	Slips of paper (or cards) with half a joke on them
Skills / Language	Speaking and listening

Preparation
Copy half a dozen jokes onto slips of paper, in halves. For example:

> Waiter, will the pancakes be long?

> No, sir. Round.

Procedure
1 As the students arrive in class, give them each a card with the first or second half of a joke written on it.

2 Ask them to memorise the words on their slip of paper.

3 Ask any student with the first half of a joke to call it out. The class listens and the student with the other half of the joke calls it out.
> **Student 1:** *Waiter, waiter, what's this fly doing in my soup?*
> **Student 2:** *Swimming, sir!*

4 Any students who need support to remember their jokes should be allowed to consult their card if they wish to.

5 When all the jokes have been heard, ask the students to recall and write down as many jokes as they can. Encourage those with good memories to help those with bad memories. Remember: this is not a test but a rapport-building task!

Variations
The students memorise their words and then get up and circulate, saying their half of the joke to other members of the class untill they find their 'other half'. If you want to change the seating arrangements, they can then sit with that person.

Instead of using jokes, you could use well-known English proverbs for this activity (e.g. *Too many cooks / spoil the broth.*). At the end of the activity, ask the students for similar proverbs in their own language.

Name Circle

Level	Any
Aim	To build rapport
Duration	10 minutes
Materials	None
Skills / Language	Speaking; vocabulary: sports, hobbies

Procedure
1 Ask the students to stand in one big circle or several smaller circles.

2 Ask them to say their name and favourite sport or hobby, making a gesture to illustrate it:
> *My name is Monica and I like cycling / swimming / playing chess.*
> (Monica mimes the activity.)

3 Ask the group to repeat the information in the third person and to imitate the action:
> *Her name is Monica and she likes cycling.*

4 Repeat for the other students in the circle.

Variations
Make this into a memory activity. The second student has to say the name and activity of the first student before they say their own:
> *Her name is Monica and she likes swimming. My name is Pedro and I like chess.*

The next person must continue in the same way, adding a name each time.

You can do this activity with other language points, depending on what you have covered with the class. Here are some other examples:
> Say your name and:
> - something you did last weekend
> - the most interesting place you've been
> - a food you like
> - a food you hate.

Back-to-back

Level	From elementary onwards
Aim	To build rapport
Duration	10 minutes
Materials	None
Skills / Language	Speaking; clothes vocabulary

Procedure

1 Tell the students to work in pairs.

2 Tell them to face their partner and look at what they are wearing. They should try to memorise as many details as possible.

3 Now ask them to stand back-to-back and describe each other's appearance.

4 Bring everyone back together as a group. Ask different students to describe their partner.

Variations

When the students have finished and are seated again, explain that you are going to describe some of the people in the class. Tell them to call out: *That's me!* when they hear themselves being described.

When they have finished the activity with each other, ask the students to remain in pairs so that one student can see you (the teacher) and one can't. Tell the student facing away from you to describe to the other what **you** are wearing.

Follow-up

Ask the students to write down as many lexical items describing clothing as they can.

Face-to-face

Level	Any
Aim	To build rapport
Duration	5 minutes
Materials	None
Skills / Language	None

Procedure

1 Put the students into pairs and tell them to stand up. Ask them to decide which person is student A and which is student B.

2 Ask them all to stand face-to-face with their partners.

3 Tell student B that they must 'mirror' every move that student A makes.

4 Demonstrate this with a student first (taking the place, momentarily, of a student B).

5 Allow student Bs a couple of minutes to 'mirror' the student As.

6 Tell the pairs to swap roles and repeat the activity.

Variations

When the activity starts, play some quiet background music while they do the 'mirroring'.

You could also do this activity in small groups (this is useful if you want the students to work in small groups afterwards). Have one person be the 'leader' while the others mirror.

NOTE: Beginning a class with a fun, non-linguistic activity like this can help break the ice between members and build rapport.

Handling Latecomers

Declaration on Lateness

At the beginning of the school year, ask the students to help you draft a Class Declaration on Lateness. You might want to do this in their own language. Make a note of what comes up. For example:

- How late is acceptable?
- What are good reasons for coming late?
- What should be the punishment, if any, for lateness?

For the next class, type up the recommendations into a Class Declaration on Lateness. Bring this to class. Read through the Declaration and ask if everyone agrees. The class sign it. You sign it yourself. Put the signed copy on the wall so that everyone can see it.

NOTE: It is vital you stick to the rules you have negotiated with the class about lateness, even (especially) if this involves yourself!

Lead-ins

It is a good idea to try to avoid beginning the lesson with the main of aims of the lesson. Start with a self-contained activity lasting, say, five minutes. This could be one of the warm-up activities described in the first section of this chapter. It is best to avoid plunging straight into your main aims. The first activity might be loosely related to the topic you will be dealing with in that lesson, but it could simply be an engaging warm-up activity.

'First Five Minute' Incentives

One way of dealing with late students is to give them an extra reason to be on time, or even early. This is more of a reward for those who aren't late, rather than a punishment for those who are. Here are three sample first-five-minute 'incentives'.

- During the first five minutes play a quick vocabulary game that the class likes and enjoys.
- When you have a test to give back to students, do it during the first five minutes of class. If someone arrives late, they get their test back at the end of the class, or even the following day (if they arrive on time!).
- During the first five minutes, tell the students that they can ask you one question about what is coming in a future test. Give them an honest answer.

If students think they are 'missing out' on something fun or important, then they might be more motivated to come on time.

The Late Seats

To avoid latecomers arriving and disrupting a class, you could set up a system whereby latecomers know where to go and what to do with minimum disruption.

- Designate two or three chairs near the door to the class as the late chairs.
- Explain that if a student comes to class late, they are to sit in these chairs so as to disrupt the class as little as possible.
- When someone comes in late, motion them to the late chair (thereby acknowledging that you have seen them) and continue with the class. Don't re-explain everything for them.

At the end of the class, talking to the student(s) in the late chairs about their lateness can help to solve the 'problem'.

How Good Is the Excuse?

Discreetly make a note of any student who comes in noticeably late.

- At the end of the class ask the latecomer to explain, in English, to the class why they were late.
- Ask the other students to be the 'judge' of how good the excuse is. If the excuse is deemed not good, then give the latecomer the 'punishment' that the class decides.

You may well find that the punishment may already have been decided if you have a Class Declaration on Lateness.

NOTE: This activity obviously only works well with classes in which students already have a good rapport with one another.

Feedback

As each wave of latecomers arrives, ask someone who was present from the beginning to summarise in some way what the lesson has been about up to that point. This could be in the form of a simple question. For example:

Can you quote one thing the teacher or one of the students has said so far?
Who can remember what we said about …?
What have we been discussing?
Can you sum up in one sentence the main point of the lesson so far?

This technique is not only useful for latecomers, it is also good to help the group focus, or refocus, on the task at hand.

Authentic Anecdote

Level	From elementary onwards
Aim	To engage students' interest
Duration	5–10 minutes
Materials	None
Skills / Language	Listening and speaking

Procedure

1 Start with an anecdote related to the theme of the lesson. For example, if the lesson is about travel, tell the class a story about a trip you have made or your daily trip to work. Keep it short.

2 Put the students in pairs and ask them to retell what they have understood to each other in English.

3 The students think of a similar anecdote and tell each other.

4 Open the coursebook and begin your lesson.

Variation

With very low-level students, you could ask them to recap what they've understood of your anecdote in their own language and then tell a similar anecdote to each other, also in their own language.

NOTE: An anecdote about you, a real person for the students, is often a more interesting way to start a lesson than an invented anecdote about an invented person in a coursebook.

Quote

Level	From elementary onwards
Aim	To engage students' interest in a topic
Duration	5 minutes
Materials	None
Skills / Language	Reading or listening

Procedure

1 Start with a quote or proverb that is related to the theme of the lesson.

2 Write the quote on the board or dictate it for one of the students to write.

3 Ask the students to translate it into their own language. Do they agree with it? What do they think?

4 Open the coursebook and begin your lesson.

Variation

Here is a variation of this activity using a quote from the news:

- Start the lesson off with a quote from someone in the news. Write or dictate the quote. (If it was originally in another language, translate it into English first.)
- Follow up by asking the students to speculate who said it and what recent news story it refers to.
- Tell them the answer.
- Now open the coursebook and begin your lesson.

Anagram

Level	From elementary onwards
Aim	To engage students' interest in a topic
Duration	5 minutes
Materials	None
Skills / Language	Vocabulary extension

Procedure

1 Take a nice long word from the day's lesson and write the letters jumbled up on the board in a big circle. For example:

```
        I   F   L
      T           S
      D           F
        U       I
          I  C  E
```

2 Ask the students how many words they can make in English using the letters on the board. They cannot repeat the same letter in an individual word. The word *difficulties* could give the following:

duties   if   fit   tie   cult   difficult
sit   fist   set   cute

3 Ask for the words that they came up with. Did anyone get a word with all the letters? If they didn't, you now tell them to open their books on the relevant page and find the word.

Questions, Questions

Level	From elementary onwards
Aim	To engage students' interest in a topic
Duration	5 minutes
Materials	None
Skills / Language	Question forms

Procedure

1 Prepare two or three questions about the theme of the lesson. Here are some example questions based on the theme of weather for a pre-intermediate class:

What's the weather today?
What's your favourite weather?
What's the coldest place you have ever been to?
Does the weather affect your feelings?

2 Write the questions on the board and ask the students to work in pairs, asking and answering the questions.

3 Do a brief feedback on this activity.

4 Open the coursebook and begin your lesson.

Variation

Give the students the theme and ask them to prepare three questions on it. Put them in pairs and tell them to ask and answer their questions.

Word Race

Level	From elementary onwards
Aim	To engage students' interest in a topic
Duration	5 minutes
Materials	None
Skills / Language	Vocabulary extension

Procedure

1 Write the topic of the lesson on the board. For example: *Music*.

2 Ask the students to work in groups and to come up with as many English words as they know about the theme within one minute. For example:

    musician   concert   CD   MP3 player   guitar

3 The group with the most words connected to the theme can come and write them on the board.

4 Open the coursebook and start the lesson.

Variation

Make a list yourself of the first ten words that come to **your** mind when you think of this topic. Don't tell the students what the words are.

- Explain that the students, in groups, will get a point for every word they write down connected with the topic, so long as you have already written it down.
- Give them a minute to brainstorm words.
- Read out your words, asking the students to cross them off their list.
- The group with the most words left can come up to the board and write them up.

NOTE: This activity can be used as an effective pre-text prediction activity. Ask the students to find how many words from the board appear in the text.

A B C Order

Level	Any
Aim	To get to know each other; rearrange seating to 'refresh' a tired class
Duration	5 minutes
Materials	None
Skills / Language	The alphabet; *What's your name? What's the first letter?*

Procedure

1 Tell the students to all stand up (with their bags, pens, etc.).

2 When they are all standing, ask them to sit in alphabetical order according to first names. Designate one place to be the 'A' seat (the first person will sit there). Tell them to do this in English.

3 If they need support, write up the following prompts to help them:

    What's your name? What's the first letter?

4 When the students have rearranged themselves, they introduce themselves to the person sitting next to them.

Variation

Ask the students to sit according to the order of their birthdays. When they have rearranged themselves, they introduce the person next to them and say their birthday.

NOTE: If you have a very big class seated in rows, simply ask the students in the same row to get in order. If you have two (or more) students with the same name, they should order themselves using the first letter of their last name.

Change Places If ...

Level	From elementary onwards
Aim	To change the seating arrangement in a class
Duration	5 minutes
Materials	None
Skills / Language	Listening; present perfect

Procedure

1 Ask the students to stand up.

2 Tell them to move and change places with another person if the sentence you are going to say is true for them.

3 Read out a series of statements, like the following:
> *Change places if you have lived in*
> *a different country.*
> *Change places if you have never swum*
> *in the ocean.*
> *Change places if you have studied English*
> *for more than a year.*
> *Change places if you have been to England.*

Variation

You can use this activity with other structures.

Present Simple
> *Change places if:*
> *you smoke*
> *you wake up late on Sundays.*

Past Simple
> *Change places if:*
> *you woke up this morning before 8 o'clock.*
> *you went out last Saturday night.*
> *you saw a movie at the weekend.*
> *you watched (a local television show) last night.*

In the Cards

Level	Any
Aim	To put students into new pairs or groups
Duration	5 minutes
Materials	A deck of playing cards
Skills / Language	Speaking; *yes / no* questions; *King, Jack, Queen, Ace, suits*

Preparation

Take out as many cards from the deck as there are students and sort them into pairs or groups.

Examples of sets in a deck of cards
Pairs
2 tens, 2 fives, 2 face cards, 2 of the same suit
Groups of three or more
the same number, the same suit

Procedure

1 Distribute the cards you have taken from the pack to the students. Elicit or teach the words for a deck of cards: *King, Queen, Jack, Ace, diamonds, hearts, clubs, spades, suits*.

2 Explain the different sets that need to work together (see examples above).

3 Tell the students to organise themselves into 'sets'.

In the Picture

Level	From elementary onwards
Aim	To organise students into groups of 3 or 4
Duration	10 minutes
Materials	Cut-up magazine pictures
Skills / Language	Speaking; *yes / no* questions

Preparation
Before class, choose pictures from a magazine and cut them into three or four pieces, according to the size of groups you want.

Procedure
1 As the students arrive for class, give them their part of the magazine picture.

2 When they are all present, explain that they have been given part of a picture. They have to circulate and find the other two or three parts of the picture to make it complete.

3 When the 'picture puzzle' is complete, they sit next to the students who make up their picture.

4 The groups tell each other what is in their picture.

Variations
The students tell each other what is in their picture without showing it.

Two groups can work together and ask each other questions to guess what the picture is about. For example:
Are there any people in the picture?
Are they inside or outside?
Are they happy or sad?
Is the weather sunny or cold?

That Odd Number: 1

Level	Any
Aim	To deal with odd numbers of students (for pairwork activities)
Duration	1 minute
Materials	None
Skills / Language	Listening to instructions

Procedure
1 Explain that you want the students to do an activity in pairs.

2 Start by assigning a group of **three** students (e.g. *Bruno, you work with Tania and Yoshi.*).

3 Now continue around the class, pairing off the others (e.g. *You two work together, you two work together.*).

4 Tell the students what they have to do for the activity.

NOTE: The odd number poses a problem for many activities in ELT, which ask for pairs or groups of four. The most common solution is to divide the class into pairs and to make one group of three. Designating the group of three **first** and **then** dividing the rest of the class into pairs avoids the all-too-common situation in which you name the pairs and finish lamely by saying something like: ... *and Miguel ... hmmm ... you work with Vera and Raquel ... OK?*

By designating the three-person group first, you reduce that sensation of being the third wheel of a bicycle for the extra student.

NOTE: This activity works equally well with groups of four and an odd number – simply begin with a group of five (or three).

That Odd Number: 2

Level	Any
Aim	To give a special role to the extra student when you have an odd number
Duration	1 minute
Materials	Role cards; dictionaries; grammar books; red and yellow cards
Skills / Language	Understanding instructions

Preparation

Have your role cards ready to give out, including red and yellow cards for the 'enforcers', and make dictionaries and grammar books available for the 'resourcers'.

Procedure

1 Divide the class into groups of four or pairs as you would normally do.

2 When you arrive at the extra person, assign them a special role, using one of the Role Cards opposite.

Variation

You can give more than one person a role. For example, in a class of thirty-six, you could have fifteen pairs and six 'spies' (or two 'spies', two 'resourcers' and two 'enforcers').

NOTE: Using these role cards has two potential advantages:
- no one feels like an 'extra'
- your pairwork activity is maintained, and possibly even enhanced.

Acknowledgement: A version of this idea first appeared in an article by Lindsay in *It's for Teachers* (volume 1, September 2001).

That Odd Number: 2 – Role Cards

The Spy

Your job is to listen carefully to the other groups and take notes of what they are saying. Write down, for example:

- any information you think is interesting or surprising
- any mistakes that you think you heard
- how many times someone spoke in a language that wasn't English.

Prepare your report for the teacher at the end of the activity.

The Enforcer

Your job is to keep a bit of order around here. To do this you can use a yellow and red card for minor and major offences! You should:

- make sure people speak only English
- make sure that people use the required language or structure (e.g. past simple)
- make sure that people don't make a certain mistake (e.g. using present simple when you need past simple)
- make sure that people are talking.

The Resourcer

You are like a walking resource for the groups. Your job is to help them if there are any words they don't know how to say. For this job you will be given a special piece of resource equipment: a dictionary or grammar book. Make sure you can use it quickly!

The Doppleganger

A doppleganger is a person who changes into another person and takes their place. In this activity you have to take someone's place! You can walk around and listen to any group or pair that you like. When you decide who you want to replace, tap them on the shoulder and show them this card. That person has to stand up and let you continue in their place. They become the new doppleganger.

Jazz Chants and Rhymes

Level	Any
Aim	To practise pronunciation, stress and rhythm
Duration	15 minutes
Materials	Jazz chants and rhymes
Skills / Language	Varied

Preparation

Choose a chant or rhyme and decide on how you are going to do it. Prepare any copies or transparencies you will need. The procedures described below can be applied to most chants and rhymes. Here we refer to the four examples of chants on page 28.

Procedure 1

Chant 1 is very simple and provides very good practice in the imperative and 'clothes' vocabulary. With a little imagination, however, you can change the language focus and even involve the pupils in creating their own chant (see Variations opposite).

1 Give out the handout of your jazz chant or put it on the board or overhead projector.

2 Say your line: *My feet hurt.*
Cue students in their line: *Take off your shoes.*
Say your next line: *My feet hurt.*
Cue students in their line: *Take off your shoes.*

3 Go though the whole text in this way, ensuring correct pronunciation, stress and rhythm.

4 Repeat without stopping, this time adopting a jazzy or rap-like rhythm. You can demonstrate this by clicking your fingers or tapping an appropriate rhythm on the desk with a ruler.

5 Encourage the students to repeat in chorus and maintain the rhythm. They can click their fingers in rhythm.

6 When they have learnt their part, withdraw the text and just prompt them by pointing to key words (e.g. *shoes, sweater, gloves*).

7 Round off the performance by asking the students to make a list of all the items of clothing and footwear that we 'put on' and 'take off'.

Variations

Ask a student to take your part (*My feet hurt*) when the class has learnt the chant.

Divide the class into those who chant *My feet hurt* and those who respond *Take off your shoes.*

Ask the students to write a parallel version of the chant, using the vocabulary items from their lists (see step 7).

Procedure 2

Chant 2 makes explicit use of the presence of boys and girls in the class.

1 If possible, put the boys and girls either sitting in two large groups or on either side of the room. If this is too disruptive, have the class sit where they always sit.

2 Provide a model for the first lines (*I've kept you waiting, I'm sorry, I'm sorry*) and get the whole class to repeat it.

3 Ask: *Who do you think is saying these words, to whom and why?* Elicit the answer *Men to women / Boys to girls on a date.*

4 Provide a model for the next part (*What's your story this time? I've been here since nine*) and get the whole class to repeat.

5 Ask: *Who is saying these lines and how do they feel?* Elicit the answer: *Girls / Women waiting for their boyfriends.*

6 Go through the whole text, getting the students to repeat in chorus.

7 Repeat the process dividing the text into Boys' and Girls' lines. Build up a rap-like rhythm. Get the students to click their fingers.

Follow-up

Get the students to write a dialogue based on the theme of the jazz chant: *Late for a date.* Begin by eliciting the excuses people make when they arrive late for a date. Put these on the board.

Get pairs of students to perform their dialogue in front of the class.

Variations

Reverse the roles: now it's the girls who have kept the boys waiting!

Use the ideas collected during the procedures to get the students to write their own version of the chant.

Jazz Chants and Rhymes

Procedure 3

In Chant 3, we have an example of a chant or rhyme created by students as a follow-up to coursebook work. In this case, the book had presented material on sport. Students were asked to write the words for an Olympics Hymn

1 Elicit or give them the first line. For example:
We can do it, we can dream

2 Put the students in groups ask them to come up with a second line to do with sport and the Olympic spirit. For example:
We can compete, we can win
or
There's a game for me and you

3 Ask the groups to come up with a line that rhymes with the previous one. For example:
We can compete, we can win
We can make it, we're all in
There's a game for me and you
There's nothing we can't do

4 Establish the rhyme pattern: a b b a.
We can do it, we can dream   a
There's a game for me and you   b
There's nothing we can't do   b
We can do it, we can dream   a

5 When the groups have finished their rhymes, collect them in.

6 In the same lesson or the next one, choose one of the texts as the jazz chant for the whole class.

Procedure 4

Chant 4 is for young learners.

1 You can give them more support by proving a near-complete text with key words missing or invite them to come up with alternative words to the original text.
In my town, there are nice places
In my town, there are nice _____
That's my town, my town's great

In my town, the _____ is clean
In my town, the grass is _____
That's my town, my town's cool

2 Get the students to perform the chant accompanied by gestures. First of all, demonstrate the gestures for the key words yourself. For example:
Nice places (point all around)
Nice faces (smile)
My town's great (thumbs up)

My town's clean (show hands, palms outwards)
Grass is green (point to something green)
My town's cool (victory sign)

Acknowledgement: Thanks to Carolyn Graham for her contribution to creative chanting in the classroom.

Jazz Chants and Rhymes

Chant 1: *My Feet Hurt*

My feet hurt
Take off your shoes
My feet hurt
Take off your shoes
My feet hurt
Take off your shoes

It's hot in here
Take off your sweater
It's hot in here
Take off your sweater
It's hot in here
Take off your sweater

My feet hurt
Take off your shoes

It's cold in here
Put on your sweater
It's cold in here
Put on your sweater

My feet hurt
Take off your shoes

My hands are cold
Put on your gloves
My hands are cold
Put on your gloves

My feet hurt
Take off your shoes

Chant 2: *The Waiting Game*

Boys: I've kept you waiting
I'm sorry, I'm sorry

Girls: What's your story this time?
I've been here since nine

Boys: Well, the car broke down
Now you're wearing a frown
Oh (baby) please say you'll forgive me today
I've kept you waiting
I'm sorry, I'm sorry

Girls: When we make a date
You're always late
I sit here and wait
While you procrastinate
Your excuses are thin
You think I'm dim
It's your car or your watch
Or you've cracked your shin

Boys: I've kept you waiting
I'm sorry, I'm sorry

Girls: Oh, be quiet and buy me a drink!

Chant 3: *Dream Team*

All: We can do it, we can dream
Girls: There's a game for me and you
Boys: There's nothing we can't do
All: We can do it, we can dream

All: We can do it, we can dream
Girls: We're playing in the same team
Boys: We're all playing to win
All: We can do it, we can dream

All: You can do it you can dream
Girls: There's only one sport, one game
Boys: Rich and poor have the same aim
All: We can do it we can dream

Chant 4: *My Town*

In my town, there are nice places
In my town, there are nice faces
That's my town, my town's great

In my town, the river is clean
In my town, the grass is green
That's my town, my town's cool

In my town, there are schools and parks
In my town, there are robins and larks
That's my town, it gets top marks

In my town, there are blue, blue skies
In my town, there are smiles in people's eyes
That's my town, it gets first prize

That's my town, my town's great
It gets top marks, it gets first prize,
My town's cool, my town's great

True for You

Level	From elementary onwards
Aim	To provide practice in pronunciation of a particular structure
Duration	5 minutes
Materials	None
Skills / Language	*To be*; adjectives

Procedure

1 Ask the students to repeat after you in chorus: *I'm from England.*

2 Ask them: *Is this true for you? Are you from England?* You should hear a chorus of *No!*

3 Tell them that you want them to repeat a sentence you say **only if it's true for them**.

4 Repeat the sentence: *I'm from England.* This time there should be silence.

5 Say: *I'm in an English class.* Everyone should repeat this time.

6 Continue like this with sentences such as the following:
I'm a student.
I'm from … (Insert a country that some / all the students are from.)
I'm tired / hungry / thirsty.
I'm thirty. (or an age of some of the students in the class)

7 Every once in a while, respond to one of the students' utterances to show you are actually listening to them and value the point of the exercise. For example:
Oh, you're hungry? Didn't you have breakfast?

Variation

You can vary this drill with other verbs or structures. For example:

Past Simple *I went to bed late last night. I watched TV.*
Have got *I've got a brother.*
Can *I can speak French.*

In some languages, the adjectives *tired*, *hungry* and *thirsty* do not go with the equivalent of *be* but rather with a verb like *have*. You can choose drills that are particularly relevant to your students.

Acknowledgement: This technique came from a workshop on drills with Paul Seligson in Granada, Spain. He had over two hundred teachers doing it, along with hoots of laughter and lots of fun.

Personal Transformation

Level	From elementary onwards
Aim	To provide practice in pronunciation of a particular structure
Duration	5 minutes
Materials	None
Skills / Language	*Like / hate / don't mind + -ing*

Procedure

1 Draw the following on the board:

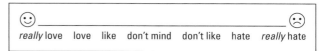

☺ _____ ☹
really love   love   like   don't mind   don't like   hate   *really* hate

2 Drill each of these words individually, paying attention to the stress on *really*.

3 Write this sentence on the board:
I like watching horror movies.

4 Read the sentence out to the students and ask them to repeat it, but making it true for themselves by changing the underlined word to one of the words in the box.

5 Tell the students you will repeat the sentence and indicate when they should say their response.

6 Repeat the sentence, allow a pause of two to three seconds, and then gesture for the whole class to say their sentences.

7 Continue the drill with sentences like the following:
I like eating fast food.
I hate dancing.
I don't mind watching football.

Variation

You can make your own drills like this for different structures and language. For example:

Conditionals *If I won the lottery, I'd …*
Relative clauses *I like people who …*
Comparatives / Superlatives *… is the best …*
… is more expensive than …

Drill Duels

Level	Any
Aim	To provide practice in pronunciation of formulaic language
Duration	5 minutes
Materials	None
Skills / Language	Varied

Procedure

1 Write the following three-line exchange on the board:
> Did you do it?
> No I didn't.
> Who did it then?

2 Ask the students to work in groups of three. Tell them to imagine a context for the dialogue. Who is speaking, where are they and what are they talking about? For example, this dialogue could be between a teacher and a boy. They could be standing in front of a broken window and the teacher wants to know who is responsible.

3 Drill the dialogue line by line. Do this a couple of times, experimenting a little with the intonation.

4 Divide the class into three groups: A, B and C. Read the first line of the dialogue and ask group A to repeat. Do the same with the second line for group B and the third line and group C.

5 Call on group A to read their line, then group B, then group C.

6 Repeat the process, making it a bit faster. Repeat again and again until you (and the class) have had enough.

7 Ask the students to write a continuation of the dialogue (another two lines). For example:
> Did you do it?
> No, I didn't.
> Who did it then?
> I don't know.
> You'd better tell me!

8 Tell the groups to present their new six-line dialogues to each other.

NOTE: As the students become more comfortable with their 'line', they will usually begin to change the intonation of their own accord.

Anchors

Level	From elementary onwards
Aim	Students find out information about everyday habits
Duration	30 minutes
Materials	Pen and paper
Skills / Language	Speaking; present simple

Procedure

1 Ask the whole class to copy the following headings from the board:
> Find someone who   Name

2 Tell the students you are going to dictate, say, seven sentences, which they should write under the first heading. For example:
> Find someone who:
> 1 has been to a Chinese restaurant.
> 2 likes Indian food.
> 3 can't stand fast food.
> 4 never eats meat.
> 5 knows how to cook spaghetti.
> 6 never has breakfast.
> 7 drinks milk before going to bed.

3 Ask half the class to stand up and the other half to remain seated.

4 Those standing up go round the room asking the questions. Whenever they get a *yes* answer, they write the name of the student in the *Name* column.

5 End the task when a student has found seven different names for their column.

6 Ask everyone to sit down.

7 To get the students to report back on the task, ask questions about the content rather than about the form. For example: *Who never has breakfast?*

8 While asking students to report back, cross-check the answers with others in the class.

NOTE: The idea is that we shouldn't completely discount 'mingle' or 'Find Someone Who' activities in large classes. Here only **half** the students move around. They can only interview those who are seated, the anchors.

Who Am I?

Level	From intermediate onwards
Aim	To discover a new 'identity'
Duration	10–15 minutes
Materials	A few small stickers with the names of famous people written on them
Skills / Language	*Yes / No* questions, in the active and passive voice

Preparation
Prepare the stickers with the names of famous people.

Procedure
1 Divide the class into two groups. One group should be towards the front and one towards the back of the room.

2 Ask one student to come and stand at the front of the class and one student to stand at the back.

3 Put a sticker on their backs with the name of a famous person written on it. For example:
   George W Bush   Tom Hanks   Einstein

4 Ask the 'famous persons' to turn round so their half of the class can see the name of the famous person on their back.

5 The 'famous persons' ask their half of the class *yes / no* questions to help them elicit who they are. For example:
   Am I dead or alive?
   Was I born in Europe?
   Am I a scientist?

6 The first half to help their famous person to guess the right answer is the winner.

7 Repeat the game with a second round, this time with two new students.

Variations
You can do the same activity as above, but with two or more students coming to the front of the class. It then becomes a whole-class activity rather than two groups competing.

For very large classes, you can do this activity as above, but in smaller groups (of five or six students). Each group nominates one person as the 'guesser'. You circulate and put the sticker on the back of each 'guesser' who quickly turns and shows the others in the group who they are. The activity then continues.

Make Your Own Questionnaire

Level	From elementary onwards
Aim	To encourage students in a large class to pay attention; to practise a grammatical structure
Duration	20 minutes
Materials	Pen and paper
Skills / Language	Present simple, past simple

Procedure
1 Dictate the following questions:
1 *How long does it take you to get to sleep at night?*
2 *How long does it take you to have a bath or shower?*
3 *How long does it take you to wash your hair?*
4 *How long does it take you to eat breakfast?*
5 *How long does it take you to get ready to go out?*

2 Ask the students to write down their answers to the questions.

3 Ask the students to work in groups of five. They ask each other the questions and write down the answers they receive.

4 Ask different students to report one interesting thing they found out from their survey.

5 In their groups, the students now write a similar questionnaire to practise the past simple, by changing the questions above and adding their own examples.

6 Students then give their questionnaire to another group to complete.

NOTE: You could keep the last part of this activity for the early finishers only.

Acknowledgement: Thanks to Mario Rinvolucri and John Morgan for the original questionnaire.

Thirty Students, Thirty Questions

Level	From elementary onwards
Aim	To build rapport; for students to find out information they'd like to know about their colleagues
Duration	20 minutes
Materials	Pen and paper
Skills / Language	Speaking

Preparation

In a class of, say, thirty, invite each student to write a question they would like to ask a friend or a person they have just met. They can write anything they like. Collect in the questions and prepare a sheet of questions based on those the students have contributed. Number the questions. For example:

1 *How would you change the design of your room?*
2 *Which items would you choose to have in your bedroom?*
3 *What are your most important possessions?*
4 *Are you a tidy person?*
5 *What do you enjoy doing in your free time?*
8 *Are you interested in protecting the environment?*
9 *Have you ever protested about something you disagree with?*
10 *What are the advantages and disadvantages of being an adolescent?*
11 *What is the ideal age to be? Why?*
12 *What kind of books do you like reading?*
13 *Which is your favourite form of transport?*
14 *What would be your ideal holiday?*
15 *Do you agree that schooldays are the best years of your life?*

Procedure

1 In the next class, nominate a student to say a number from 1–30.

2 Read out the question of the number chosen and tell the class they have thirty seconds to talk about the question. They should do this in pairs (with the person next to them).

3 Nominate a student to answer the question and signal to the class to listen to the answer.

4 The student then calls out another student by name and says a different number. Repeat the process.

NOTE: You could do a few of these each day, depending on the number of students you have in the class. The students have to pay attention as the numbers cannot be repeated.

Tongue-tied

Level	From elementary onwards
Aim	To build rapport; to discuss topics that interest the students
Duration	30 minutes
Materials	Slips of paper
Skills / Language	Speaking

Procedure

1 Ask the students to write down on a slip of paper the topics they would ideally like to talk about in class or if they were being interviewed on TV. For example, they might write:

The ideal partner
The best way to deal with the drug problem
My ideal house
My ideal holiday

2 Collect in the slips of paper.

3 Tell the students they are going to prepare a talk on one of the following topics. Read out a selection of the topics they have contributed to the pool.

4 Ask students to agree on one topic.

5 Give them time to work in pairs or groups to brainstorm ideas on the topic they have chosen.

6 Divide the class into large groups: A and B (draw an invisible line down the middle of the class).

7 Nominate a student (at random) from one half of the class, group A, to start talking about the topic.

8 After about thirty seconds, stop the student and call out another name at random from the other half of the class, group B. That student then continues from where the previous student left off.

9 After thirty seconds, call out the name of a student from group A to continue from where the previous student left off.

10 Continue until one of the groups becomes tongue-tied.

11 Repeat the process with another topic chosen from the student-generated list.

Backs Turned

Level	From elementary onwards
Aim	To practise describing a picture
Duration	10 minutes
Materials	A large magazine picture or wall chart
Skills / Language	Speaking

Procedure

1 Divide the class into pairs and ask one student from each pair to face the back of the class.

2 Show a picture to the half of the class facing you. The students have to describe the picture to the partner who has his / her back turned. Those with their backs turned can ask *yes / no* questions to try to elicit information from the partner who can see the picture.

Variations

If you want to reduce the noise level, ask the class do the activity as two large groups, rather than, say, twenty pairs.

You can also post a different picture on the back wall and create an 'information gap' / 'spot the difference' activity.

The Best Memory

Level	From intermediate onwards
Aim	To encourage students in a large class to pay attention; to practise a grammatical structure
Duration	10 minutes
Materials	None
Skills / Language	Grammatical structures (here, the present perfect)

Procedure

1 Decide on the model structure you want to practise. Elicit ideas for a particular topic. For example: *holidays, crime.*

2 Ask one or two students to write ideas on the board as they come up.

3 When you have enough ideas, nominate a student who will keep count of how many sentences are remembered.

4 Ask a student to say a sentence on the model. For example:
> *My name's X and I've never (been to Italy).*
> *I've never committed a burglary …*

5 Ask another student to repeat what the first one said and add their own example sentence.

6 Ask a third student to repeat what the previous student said and to add their own example.

7 Continue until a student makes a mistake.

8 Begin another chain, using different students and repeat the process.

9 At the end of the activity, declare a winner. Who remembered the most sentences?

Follow-up

Ask the students to write down as much information as they can remember, based on the activity they've just completed.

Variation

For beginners, you can use the following model which uses the present simple. Students say their name and anything they like beginning with the same letter as their initial:
> *My name is Luke and I like lemons.*
> *My name is Sue and I like strawberries.*
> *My name is Matthew and I like mushrooms.*

The other students repeat:
> *His name is Luke and he likes lemons.*
> *Her name is Sue and she likes strawberries.*
> *His name is Matthew and he likes mushrooms.*

Ping-pong Speaking

Level	From elementary onwards
Aim	To exchange personal information
Duration	5–15 minutes
Materials	Topic cards; slips of paper
Language / Skills	Speaking

Preparation
Prepare a list of interesting topics to talk about (e.g. dreams, the future, an ideal weekend, morning routines) on cards and slips of paper for students to write on. Each student should have at least two slips of paper.

Procedure
1 Write up the topics on the board and make sure the students understand them.

2 Ask the students to take two or three slips of paper and write a question on each one. The question should be something they would like to ask their partner or be asked by them. The question can relate to any of the topics. Give them a few examples:

What was your last dream about?
Where would you like to spend your ideal weekend?
What is the first thing you do in the morning when you wake up?

3 Collect the students' slips of paper and put them into two piles face down on a table at the front of the class.

4 The students form two teams: A and B. Ask them to stand on either side of the table in a row behind their pile of questions.

5 Player 1 in team A takes a slip of paper and reads out the question. Player 1 in team B has to answer the question in one or two sentences (not one word!). If questions are badly formed or incorrect, correct them orally and ask the student to repeat the correct version.

6 Player 1 in team B then takes a slip and reads out the question. Player 1 in team A has to answer the question in one of two sentences (not one word!).

7 Player 2 in team A repeats the process with player 2 in team B, and so on.

8 A point is awarded for every question answered appropriately, i.e. in one or two sentences. Failure to answer or an answer made up only of one word or short phrase, does not earn the player a point.

NOTE: For groups bigger than thirty students, you may wish to form two subgroups and run both games simultaneously.

Half a Minute!

Level	From intermediate onwards
Aim	To provide practice in fluency
Duration	15 minutes
Materials	Topic cards; a watch
Language / Skills	Speaking

Preparation
Prepare a list of interesting topics to talk about on cards.

Procedure
1 Divide the class into two teams: A and B.

2 Explain the rules of the game: you are going to give the students a topic to talk about for half a minute (chosen from your collection of 'topics-to-talk-about'). For example:

rock music	women drivers	free time
money	love	

3 The first player in either team who volunteers to talk about the topic must do so for half a minute without changing the subject or repeating him / herself. If the opposing team think the speaker has changed the subject (i.e. is 'waffling') or is repeating him / herself, they may 'challenge'.

4 If the challenge is accepted by the referee (i.e. you, the teacher), the challenging team then continues the topic for the rest of the half minute.

5 Whoever completes the half minute successfully earns a point for their team.

6 Continue playing until one team reaches ten points (or you or the students are tired of the game).

Take Up the Story

Level	From elementary onwards
Aim	To provide practice in fluency
Duration	15 minutes
Materials	None
Language / Skills	Past tenses; speaking

Procedure

1 Divide the students into small groups of three, four or five.

2 Explain that they are going to tell a story together in turns. First, they must decide on a topic. This could be based on their own experience or on a story they have read or heard. For example: *Something that happened to me yesterday.*

Note that they should only decide on the topic – not plan the story! Tell them that this is an exercise requiring them to think on their feet in English.

3 Ask them to number off the students in their group as Narrator 1, Narrator 2, etc.

4 Tell Narrator 1 to start off.

5 At random points in the narrative, you give a signal: *Take it up!*

6 Narrator 2 takes up the story exactly where Narrator 1 left off.

7 At another random point, you again give the signal: *Take it up!*

8 Narrator 3 takes up the story from where Narrator 2 left off

9 The story continues in turns, with Narrator 1 taking up the story after the last person in the group has finished.

10 The process continues for as long as you have time and the students have motivation.

Variation

This can be done as a game in front of the class with five or six students standing or sitting in a straight line and telling a story, sentence by sentence. The players are eliminated when they fail to come up with a continuation to the story. The winner is the person who can keep the story going the longest without drying up.

Why?

Level	From intermediate onwards
Aim	To provide practice in fluency and to encourage students to listen to each other
Duration	15 minutes
Materials	None
Language / Skills	Question formation; speaking and listening

Procedure

1 Ask the students to work in pairs or small groups. Tell them to nominate a Narrator.

2 The Narrator has to prepare to tell a story based on their own experience or a story they have read or heard. The story should take about five minutes to tell. For example: *A terrible holiday*

3 Ask the Narrator to start the story.

4 At random points in the narrative, the listener(s) can interrupt and ask *Why?*

5 The Narrator has to find an answer. Any answer is acceptable as long as it is in English. For example:

Narrator *… and then I bought a bar of chocolate …*
Listener *Why (did you buy the chocolate)?*
Narrator *Because I love chocolate. And anyway, when I got home I was feeling very tired …*
Listener *Why?*
Narrator *Because I had done a lot of shopping …*

6 The Narrator continues until they finish the story or you call *Stop!* (when you feel they've had enough). Then a different student becomes the Narrator for the group.

7 At the end of the activity, ask how many Narrators could finish their story. Can other people in the group remember what the different stories were about?

What Did We Do Today?

Level	Any
Aim	To revise what you have done in the lesson
Duration	5 minutes
Materials	None
Skills / Language	Varied

Procedure

1 As you come to the end of the lesson, ask the students to close their books or turn their pages over.

2 Put them in pairs ask them to tell each other as much as they can remember about the lesson they have just had. They can do this in their own language if they need to.

3 Conduct a whole-class feedback session in English and ask different pairs to report.

Variation

To make this more focused, ask the students to finish the following sentences as if they were writing to a colleague who had missed the class:

If you missed today's class:
– you should read (page 00 in the book, a certain handout)
– you should do (exercises X, Y, Z in the book, the workbook)
– you should remember (important things that came up, new words).

NOTE: With lower levels, students could do this in their own language.

Future Test Questions

Level	Any
Aim	To revise what you have done; to prepare for a future test
Duration	10 minutes
Materials	None
Skills / Language	Varied

Procedure

1 Ask the students to work in pairs and come up with one test question on the lesson they have just had. To help them, provide examples of test question types like the following:

Test Question Types

Multiple Choice
Complete the sentence with the correct word.
Last night we _____ to the cinema.
a) went
b) have gone
c) go

Sentence Transformation
Change the sentence from the active to the passive.
The police stopped the demonstration.
The demonstration _____ .

Sentence Completion
Complete the sentence with a word.
I'm not afraid ___ spiders.

Odd Word Out
Which of the following words does not belong?
green   yellow   under   black   blue

2 Ask four or five pairs to read out their questions. Elicit the answers from other pairs.

3 Make a note of some of these questions and incorporate them into the next test. Inform the students that you are going to do this.

Word of the Day

Level	Any
Aim	To revise vocabulary covered in the lesson
Duration	5 minutes
Materials	None
Skills / Language	New words learnt in class

Procedure

1 Ask the students to suggest a 'word of the day' for that day's lesson. This could be a word that:

- students think is useful to know
- students like
- students think sounds strange
- is difficult to pronounce
- is related to the lesson but didn't come up
- is strange, funny or topical.

2 Write the word on the board and make a note of it yourself to use in future quizzes or tests.

NOTE: You can find several websites that offer Words of the Day. For example:

Oxford English Dictionary word of the day: http://www.oed.com/cgi/display/wotd

The New York Times word of the day: http://www.nytimes.com/learning/students/wordofday

Merriam Webster: http://www.wordcentral.com and follow the links to the buzzword

Don't Smile!

Level	Any
Aim	To end the lesson on a high note
Duration	5 minutes
Materials	None
Skills / Language	None

Procedure

1 Ask the students to stand face-to-face with a partner, making eye contact but keeping a 'straight face'.

2 Eliminate any pair in which either partner smiles.

3 The 'winner' is the last person or pair to keep a straight face.

Variation

This activity also makes a good warm-up. Whether as an ice-breaker or as a cool-down, the activity is relatively quiet.

Acknowledgement: This activity is based on an idea by Charlyn Wessels.

Body Dictation

Level	Any
Aim	To end the lesson on a high note
Duration	1 minute
Materials	None
Skills / Language	Listening; imperatives

Procedure

1 At the end of lesson, explain that you are going to give a special dictation to test listening skills. The students have to listen carefully and do every action you say.

2 Begin with an example:
   Lift your right hand in the air.

3 Once everyone has the idea, continue:
   Pick up your pen with your right hand.
   Put your pen away.
   Pick up your book(s) with both hands.
   Put your books away.
   Stand up.
   Turn to the person next to you.
   Say 'It was nice to see you today.'
   Say 'See you next class.'
   Take your bags.
   Turn and look at me.
   Say 'Goodbye!'

4 When the students all say goodbye, say goodbye to them and indicate that the class is finished (e.g. by picking up your things).

Exit Music

Level	Any
Aim	To end the lesson on a high note; to 'close' the English classroom space
Duration	1 minute
Materials	A recording with 'theme music' for the end of the lesson
Skills / Language	None

Preparation

Choose your music and have it in place, ready to switch on, so that you don't have to go searching for the right piece at the time and ruin the effect.

Procedure

1 Wait until the last activity of the lesson is winding down (perhaps three or four minutes before the end) and discreetly put on the music and leave the volume quite low.

2 Circulate and monitor the class for a minute or so while they finish.

3 Call the class to attention to finish the activity. Thank them and tell them the lesson is over.

4 As everyone starts putting things away, slowly turn the music up more. Leave the music on as they all leave the classroom.

NOTE: This can be particularly helpful if you have trouble bringing a class to a smooth end. Think of films you have seen, you always know when it's over because of the music!

2

Discipline Problems

'I just can't handle them anymore!'

Discipline is probably the number one concern of many teachers. It was one of the principal 'difficulties' we had in mind when writing this book. You will find that, inevitably, other chapters touch on aspects of teaching that contribute to reducing discipline problems. But sometimes, whatever we seem to try, the students just refuse to behave! This chapter takes a closer look at what a discipline problem is, why it occurs and what to do about it. As one teacher friend remarked, 'You wouldn't believe the things they get up to …'

A discipline problem can be defined as any action, overt or covert, that undermines the unity or cohesion of the class. Here are some examples of misbehaviour that we have encountered. We're sure you can think of more.

Overt
- shouting
- asking to leave the room repeatedly
- muttering rude remarks or swearing in class
- cheeky remarks to the teacher
- chewing gum
- refusing to do set work or homework
- fighting others in class
- scribbling on books
- questioning the usefulness of tasks and or the teacher's competence

Covert
- not paying attention
- arriving late
- missing lessons
- talking when meant to be writing
- clicking pens or dropping things
- sighing noisily
- leaning back in / rocking on chairs
- looking out of the window or across the room
- packing up early, as if to leave
- keeping books closed
- asking to change the activity, for example to a song

The lists above suggest that 'discipline' is a complex problem and can take a number of different forms which are not always obvious. Many teachers may not realise they even have a discipline problem because they tend to assume only overt kinds of disruption (shouting out, refusing to co-operate) are real discipline problems. Both forms of 'indiscipline' are signs that students are not paying the kind of attention you would like and are, by their actions, also undermining the 'togetherness' of the group and the idea of working collectively towards common aims.

As discipline problems and their causes are so varied and elusive, it is probably easier to define the absence of a discipline problem rather than its existence. When you can get students' attention and keep it (for the duration of a lesson) then it is safe to say you do not have discipline problems.

We all have our own way of dealing, or not dealing, with a discipline problem. There are many variables such as age, environment and cultural background. Some classes have discipline problems because they have not gelled properly. And as every teacher knows, there are always some days when nothing goes right!

There **are** strategies and activities that can address discipline problems, however, and help to remove them before they even come into existence or to resolve them when they do make an appearance.

2.1 Diffusing Discipline

'When Ms K. came into the room, she seemed very serious. She didn't try to be friendly, like some teachers, but we always respected her. She waited for everybody to be quiet.' (10-year-old pupil)

This section offers some strategies to help you to establish a sense of rule-based behaviour and teacher presence from the early stages of a new class and to avoid discipline problems before they become problems.

As with any public appearance, first impressions are vital in winning over your audience of students. And they continue to be of fundamental importance throughout the course as you and your students work together.

2.2 Rules and Regulations

'They show no respect for the rules.'

In the second section, you will find activities for drawing up rules and regulations with the students' involvement in order to create a sense of ownership of these rules. The traditional and still pertinent response to discipline problems in class is on the level of rules and regulations, or the question of what students are allowed to do, what they are obliged to do and what the official sanctions are for failing to abide by these rules. However, if students feel they 'own' the rules they are more likely to uphold them

and resent those who violate them. Peer pressure on unruly pupils is potentially one of the teacher's greatest allies in combating indiscipline.

2.3 Raising Awareness

'If they only knew how it felt ...'

The activities in the third section help you raise awareness of discipline problems with your students and, together, come up with solutions.

If you are creating rules and regulations with the students' involvement, it is worth canvassing their opinions on discipline and discipline problems, too. Many students will have their own feelings about discipline and how to deal with it. Even very young students have a clear idea of what is fair and unfair.

2.4 Building Good Behaviour

'If only I knew why they misbehaved.'

Why students misbehave is, of course, the $65,000,000 dollar question. It is one that even students themselves, when interviewed about misbehaviour, don't always know the answer to.

For many theorists of motivation such as Abraham Maslow, self-esteem is one of the driving forces behind all learning. Self-esteem is something we can encourage in an immediate sense through our everyday practice. Maslow, however, also refers to self-actualisation as a powerful motivating factor in learning, but this is a long-term aim of all learning. It is not easy for teachers in the everyday circumstances of most teaching situations to see how they can contribute to another human being's fulfillment, personal or professional. But we can at least begin to build motivation by working on the lower and simpler levels of Maslow's pyramid.

Maslow's Hierarchy of Needs

We need to notice that in Maslow's scheme there are fundamental issues to address even before students can be motivated to learn. These are:

- the need to feel physically comfortable (the room should not be too hot or too cold; they should not feel hungry, thirty or wish to go to the toilet!)
- the need to feel safe, both physically and mentally
- the need to feel they belong in the group.

These are all things that should be dealt with early on in any course. The activities in this section help to build students' self-esteem.

2.5 Discipline-friendly Tasks

'This is all very well, but sometimes I just need them to be quiet!'

The activities in this section build on the principles of creativity and collaboration in written work, while integrating it with other skills.

In the language classroom, some techniques encourage good discipline (they are 'discipline-friendly') and other techniques, however interesting and relevant they might be, may have a tendency to disrupt the class (they are 'discipline-unfriendly').

Team quiz games, group work and pairwork are classroom activities that can easily become discipline-unfriendly. We are not advocating you use only discipline-friendly activities, but it is true that every once in a while you need a break.

Writing and dictations are what we call 'discipline-friendly' activities and with large classes this is especially true. The moment of glorious silence (bar the sound of pencils scratching) gives the teacher a much-needed break. Although they are often considered as traditional, boring activities, they needn't be. Dictations can be very rich activities if the teacher knows how to take full advantage of them.

2.6 An Element of Surprise

'Sometimes I think they act up because they're bored. I need to 'shake them up' a bit but I don't know how.'

The activities in the final section contain an element of surprise that might 'soothe even the most savage of beasts'. Variety in your classes, and surprise, can also make even traditionally discipline-unfriendly activities work. Have you ever thought of setting up a competitive quiz (which might make the students go crazy) but having the school director come in and act as judge of points and answers?

The problem with the 'quality' of good teaching is that it is very elusive and yet we all know it when we see it. We see it in our favourite actors, that quality that attracts attention and makes you want to look at or listen to somebody – and to go on looking and listening. How can we as teachers benefit from the 'Al Pacino' or 'Meryl Streep' factor?

The list below shows the results of research into what makes a good teacher.

Qualities
1 friendly
2 explains well
3 has a sense of humour
4 knows the subject
5 is patient
6 is kind
7 believes in students
8 is interesting
9 talks about other things
10 is enthusiastic

These are features that help give a teacher 'presence' and thereby reduce discipline problems. There is no correct order, but you might like to stop and think for a moment how many of these qualities you have – and which ones you could work on more to get that 'X' factor in teaching.

Diffusing Discipline

First and Foremost
Always remember: the best attention-getter is the sheer force of your personality, your presence.

The First Encounter
As with any performance (and a part at least of teaching involves an element of performing), the first few minutes are vital in establishing the right kind of expectations of what is to follow. You must make the most of those first crucial moments. Prepare yourself:

- Get there first, introduce yourself and familiarise yourself with who's sitting where.
- Discover and use the students' names.
- Scan the class to get attention, stop mid-sentence, wait, look steadily.
- Wait for silence and use it effectively: *I'd like you all to look this way and listen carefully.*
- Vary your style through careful use of:
  voice   tone   pitch   facial expression   posture
  use of space   proximity
- Set the boundaries. This means telling the students what you expect from them in terms of behaviour.
- Give the lesson a clear form and state it. Make your targets achievable.
- Use *we*.
- Use repetition and the settling power of positive routine.
- Make sure preparation, including timing, is apparent.
- Give the overall impression: *I am relaxed and confident.*

Teachers who come to class unprepared, who don't learn the students' names, who aren't confident in front of the class, tend to make a bad first impression. They subsequently run the risk of having discipline problems. You don't have to be one of them.

Further Encounters
It is not enough to get attention: we have got to try to maintain attention throughout a lesson or series of lessons. Here are some tips for maintaining discipline as you get to know a class better:

- Remember that a fresh and vigorous approach engages students' attention.

- Plan your movements: give warnings of changes in activities.
- Show how content is related to students' interests, existing knowledge and future concerns.
- Vary activities and learning styles.
- Distribute attention equally. Be flexible enough to value unexpected contributions.
- Keep a roving eye: show that everything is noticed, even if intervention is avoided.
- Keep up the momentum, vary the pace. Don't interrupt the flow of a lesson unnecessarily.
- Be aware of your space: front, back and the sides.

If you can keep students' attention on you, on the task at hand or on each other then there's a greater chance of learning taking place. Your life is also much easier.

Feeling Good, Working Better
If we recognise that self-esteem is important, then it's up to us to try to make students feel good about their work, however imperfect, and by extension, themselves. Here are some suggestions:

- Use *I* rather than *you* statements.
- Help students accomplish something and contribute to the group.
- Make it clear you care for and respect the person.
- Sit or crouch next to, rather than tower over, students – especially children.
- Show you care when someone is absent.

These techniques, which successful teachers use from the very beginning to help build and maintain students' self-esteem, may pre-empt discipline problems before they take shape.

A Rewarding System
A built-in system of rewards provides extrinsic motivation for students to behave better. This is also what is called the 'carrot' approach to discipline in the classroom. For example:

- giving gold stars for children (and why not adults?) for work well done
- ending the lesson with a game or a song
- tossing a sweet to a student who has given a good answer (this also makes the prohibited act of eating in class a rare treat for work well done)
- giving a 'hint' or advice about an upcoming exam
- giving certificates for younger learners, which could be sent home for parents or displayed on the wall
- giving a special class reward, like a trip or excursion somewhere

- showing a video that the students choose, or arranging a trip to the computer room (both, if your school has the facilities)
- making a phone call or writing home (this is usually reserved for bad behaviour in children, but can have an extremely beneficial effect if used for good behaviour).

The advantage of using rewards is that one kind of sanction can involve withholding or postponing them (see Sanctions below). Making motivating group rewards dependant on good group behaviour will also mean that the group itself will punish misbehaviour of its members without you having to do anything.

A Real Reward

Bob Dylan says in one of his songs (Love Minus Zero) *there's no success like failure* and we had often wondered what this puzzling statement could mean. In the context of dealing with difficulties in the classroom, and discipline in particular, we can interpret the statement as one way of stressing the importance of success in learning.

- Take every opportunity to reward students for their efforts. This turns into practical pedagogic terms the old adage that 'nothing succeeds like success'.
- Communicate the feeling of achievement in having completed a task successfully. This is more important than a gold star to stick on the notebook or a sweet from the teacher.
- Encourage students in the things you say to them (*Well done!*) and the **way** you say them (our voice can be in itself a reward or a reprimand for students).

If we can transform the habit of failure into an opportunity for success, this will have added value in terms of language learnt but, even more, in terms of learning to believe in oneself.

Sanctions

In spite of the previous batch of optimistic strategies, sometimes you may still have to 'punish' in order to instil in the learners a greater sense of responsibility for their own actions. If the rewards are the carrot, sanctions are the 'stick'. They vary, from the minimal (a verbal reprimand or even a mere frown from the teacher) to the draconian (expulsion from the classroom or school, achieved through the use of the institutional authority of the director or head teacher).

Here is a checklist for building reasonable and logical sanctions into your teaching:

- Use eye contact as the first warning. A hard stare can be quite effective. Stare and shift eye contact.
- If behaviour doesn't change, try the discreet approach. Soft, private reprimands are often better than noisy public rebuke.
- Use individual students' names and specify unwanted behaviour. Make corrective statements short (*Stefan, you're chewing gum in class. Please take it out.*).
- Refer to the group's established rules, especially if you've designed them together (see section on Rules and Regulations).
- Establish peace clearly and explicitly before moving on.
- If you send someone out, do it with clear and achievable terms for re-entry, such as *Come back in five minutes* or *Tell me when you are ready to come back.*
- If you punish someone and it turns out to be unjustified, admit your mistake and give generous apologies.
- Prepare a strong ending to your lesson, to be stuck to after disruption.
- End on a smile whatever sanctions you have been obliged to implement.

It is vital in adopting any strategy with sanctions that we make sure 'the punishment fits the crime'.

Acknowledgement: Thanks to M McManus for some of the ideas in this section.

Let's Make a Contract

Level	Any
Aim	To encourage a sense of ownership of class rules
Duration	30 minutes
Materials	Pen and paper
Language / Skills	Modal verbs of obligation

Preparation

Draw up your own preferred rules of classroom behaviour.

Procedure

1 Refer to a disciple problem that has come up recently in your class. For example: shouting out, chewing, arriving late for class.

2 Show the students **your** version of possible class rules, including your own obligations to the class. For example:

1 *Students should not chew in class.*
2 *Students must listen to each other respectfully.*
3 *Students must do all their homework.*
4 *Students should always bring their textbooks and a notebook to write in.*
5 *I will start and end classes promptly.*
6 *I will return the homework promptly.*
7 *I will not threaten students.*
8 *I will treat all students fairly.*

3 Tell the students that they are going to draw up a contract. Put them into groups to prepare the first draft of **their** contract. They should list up to ten points.

4 Mix members of the different groups and get them to pool their ideas. They should select up to ten rules that they think are the most important. For example:

1 *We will try to speak in English.*
2 *We will not disturb other students.*
3 *We will always bring our books, pens and a notebook.*
4 *We will listen carefully when the teacher is speaking.*
5 *We will be quiet (and listen) when someone else is speaking.*
6 *We will do our homework on time.*
7 *We will arrive in the classroom a few minutes early.*
8 *We will not eat or chew gum in class.*
9 *We will leave the room quietly at the end of the class.*
10 *We will respect the teacher and the other students.*

5 The students can include a section in their contract stating their (reasonable) expectations of the teacher. For example:

1 *The teacher will speak to us respectfully.*
2 *The teacher will correct our homework on time.*
3 *The teacher will arrive on time.*
4 *The teacher will give us advance notice of all tests.*
5 *The teacher will remember what we did in the previous lesson.*

6 When they have finished, go through the final version. If there are any rules you want to add, do so now. Explain to the class the rules you want to add and why.

7 Take away the contract and type it up (or copy it out so it looks like a 'real' contract).

8 Display it somewhere visible in the classroom. If you are unable to do this (e.g. you are not allowed to stick paper on the walls), then make copies for all the students in the class and ask them to stick the contract on the first page of their notebook.

9 If there is a breach of rules in class and you need to call students' attention to it, remind them that this was a rule they agreed on in their contract.

Variation

As part of the contract, you can also negotiate what the sanctions will be for not respecting the rules.

NOTE: This process of drawing up a contract can be done in the students' own language. The contract is also something which can be revisited and updated (see next activity).

Class Contract, Version 2

Level	Any
Aim	To re-evaluate classroom rules with students
Duration	20 minutes
Materials	Your original class contract (see Let's Make a Contract above)
Language / Skills	Modal verbs of obligation

Preparation

Make copies of the original class contract (see Let's Make a Contract on page 44) for every four or five students.

Procedure

1 Two or three months after you've made a class contract, ask the students how many rules they can remember from the original contract and elicit examples from the class.

2 Ask the students to work in small groups. Explain that you would like them to look at the classroom contract and:
- put a tick next to the rules that are working
- put a cross next to the rules that aren't working
- make any suggestions for other rules they think necessary.

3 Give each group a copy of the original class contract and let them get to work.

4 Take advantage of this time to think about your own recommendations. Decide if there are any **you** would like to change, add or delete.

5 Mix members of the different groups and ask them to compare their ideas.

6 Have a whole-class discussion about what rules they think are working, what rules aren't working and any new rules they'd like to add. Give your own ideas as well during the discussion. Take notes of any changes and go through all the suggested changes at the end of the activity.

7 Take your notes and use them to draft a new contract. This is Contract Version 2. Put it on the wall where the students can see it.

8 You can repeat this activity at different stages of the year (e.g. at the beginning of each term).

NOTES: Class contracts are useful tools but sometimes they get lost, forgotten or simply outdated. It is a useful exercise to revisit them, even if there haven't been any major breaches of the rules. That way you can suggest deleting some rules because they are no longer necessary (i.e. because the students are behaving so well!).

This process of revisiting a contract can be done in the students' own language.

Brainstorm

Level	Any
Aim	To find a solution to a particular discipline problem
Duration	20 minutes
Materials	Pen and paper
Language / Skills	Suggestions: *I think we should ... , Why don't we ...?*

Procedure

1 Make a clear statement of a problem. For example: a student has not done any homework for a long time.

2 Initiate a class discussion by asking questions, listening reflectively, probing, clarifying issues, restating the problem and possible solutions.

3 Ask the students to get into groups and brainstorm ideas for solving the problem. Tell them to make notes.

4 In turn, each group suggests their preferred solution(s) to the problem to the rest of the class. For example:
  1 *A rule should be agreed on for the minimum number of assignments students are expected to complete each term.*
  2 *After a certain number of uncompleted assignments, the offender will be asked to sit outside the classroom and complete the latest assignment.*
  3 *The offender can be 'tutored' by another student to help him or her complete the missing assignments.*

5 The class chooses, for example, the top three solutions and makes a plan to implement them, monitor their progress and agree when to review and evaluate the situation.

6 Evaluate the success of the solution after the agreed trial period.

Bad Teacher, Good Teacher

Level	From intermediate onwards
Aim	To raise awareness about varieties of discipline and possible teacher reactions
Duration	30 minutes
Materials	None
Language / Skills	Present simple

Preparation

Make copies of different situations (see below), one for every pair of students.

Situations

A student's mobile phone rings.

Two students are passing notes at the back of the class.

A student says something rude to another student.

A student says something rude to the teacher.

Two minutes before the end of the class, everybody puts their books in their bags. The teacher is still giving class.

A student always shouts out the answer to the teacher's questions. He / She doesn't let other students answer.

A student is playing with a Gameboy in class.

(You can add other situations that are pertinent or problematic in your class.)

Procedure

1 Ask the students to work in pairs. Name each pair as an A pair or a B pair.

2 Give the example of the following situation:
   A student is speaking while the teacher is speaking. The teacher wants the student to stop and listen.

3 Ask the A pairs to brainstorm what a 'bad' teacher would do in that situation. They can base this on previous experience they've had. They should write down one or two things. Tell the B pairs to brainstorm what a 'good' teacher would do and write in on the paper.

4 Distribute the copies of situations below and ask the students to do the same for the situations above.

5 When they have finished, put the students in groups: an A pair with a B pair. Ask them to compare their answers.

6 Do some whole-class feedback. Make notes on the board as you elicit the feedback from the As and the Bs.

The Bad Teacher ...	The Good Teacher ...
• shouts	• doesn't lose his / her temper
• ignores the student and continues talking	• asks the student a question
• gives an unfair punishment	• thanks the student when he / she stops talking
• gets angry at the class.	• asks for silence respectfully.

7 Collect the written notes and read out individual points at random and ask students to say whether they are what the bad or good teacher would do and why.

NOTE: You could do an activity like this **before** making a contract (see page 44). It will also give you an idea of what kind of teacher behaviour, in the face of discipline problems, the students react badly to!

Act It Out

Level	Any
Aim	To raise awareness of the disruptive effect of some behaviour
Duration	10 minutes
Materials	Slips of paper with instructions (see Preparation)
Language / Skills	Imperatives; modals: *must* / *should*

Preparation

Write down recent forms of 'misbehaviour' and prepare the slips. Make enough for a dozen or so students. For example:

Shout out all the answers.
Speak in your own language all the time.
Get up and leave the room.
Keep clicking your pen.
Look out of the window.
Talk loudly to your partner while another student is speaking.

Procedure

1 Give out the instruction slips to about a dozen students. Tell them:
- they should not show this slip to anybody else
- they should follow the instruction on the slip when the lesson gets underway.

2 Tell the class you're going to teach the lesson as normal but as you do so the class should try to notice any unusual behaviour on the part of other members of the class.

3 Conduct the lesson as you would normally do. Signal that 'the lesson is now starting'.

4 Stop after about 15 minutes and elicit what the 'disruptive' students were doing. For example:
Maria was getting up all the time.
Peter was clicking his pen.
John was looking out of the window.

5 Write these on the board.

6 Ask the students what effect this behaviour had on the class. For example:
We couldn't concentrate.
We couldn't hear what was going on.
We didn't get much work done.

7 Ask students to sum up the implications of the activity by writing 'rules'. For example:
We shouldn't shout out.
We mustn't click our pens all the time.

Surprise Tactics

Level	Any
Aim	To consider the implications of misbehaviour in class
Duration	5 minutes
Materials	Sweets; gum pens
Language / Skills	Varied

Procedure

1 Establish which kind of misbehaviour is persistent, as in the activity Act It Out opposite. For example:
chewing   clicking pens
talking while others are talking

2 Try the following 'surprise tactics':
- When a student gets a question right, give them a sweet or some gum till the whole class is chewing. When the session is over, go round with a bin and 'collect' the gum. Ask: *What impression do a lot of people eating sweets or chewing gum have on you?*
- Ask the students to pick up their pens and click them all together for fifteen seconds. When the clicking session is over, ask them to put their pens down. Ask: *What effect does pens clicking in the background have on your concentration and cohesion as a class?*
- Stop the lesson mid-flow and ask everyone to talk to their partner. Stop this 'talk session' after fifteen seconds. Ask: *What effect does this kind of noise have on the flow of the lesson?*

3 To highlight and add humour to other types of misbehaviour, try 'exaggerating' the behaviour, followed by reflection on its consequences. For example:
Everybody look out of the window.
Everybody lean back in your chair and start rocking.
Everybody shout out the answer to the next question.

4 Round off by asking the students to make their own list of 'disruptive activities'. How many can they come up with? Can they order them into serious / less serious?

Write All About It

Level	From intermediate onwards
Aim	To raise awareness of discipline problems, their causes and possible solutions
Duration	5–10 minutes (in class) one hour (at home)
Materials	Pen and paper
Language / Skills	Passive voice: *X is caused by …;* expressing cause and effect; suggesting solutions; modal verbs: *can, could*

Procedure

1 After a disruptive incident (when the students have had time to calm down), brainstorm three paragraphs for a composition entitled *Discipline Problems in School*. For example:

1 Examples of Indiscipline	2 Causes	3 Solutions
shouting out	Students like to show off.	We could draw up a set of rules.
not paying attention	They want attention.	We could make punishment more severe.
arriving late	They are under pressure.	We could make classes more motivating

2 Ask the students to write up their composition for homework, adding to the ideas brainstormed in class.

Variation

Make a poster or mind-map of the ideas resulting from the brainstorming session and display them on the wall.

Class Helpers

Level	From elementary onwards
Aim	To give roles and a sense of ownership of what happens in class
Duration	Not applicable
Materials	None
Language / Skills	Instructions

Preparation
Prepare cards with the Helper 'roles' on them (optional).

Procedure
1 At the beginning of the school week, assign different roles to different students to help you with the class. See opposite for some roles you can assign and the responsibilities they might entail.

2 Explain what the responsibilities of this person are and make sure they understand. You could give them a special role card for the week. For example:

You are the messenger this week.
Your responsibilities include:
- giving out students' work and collecting it
- taking messages outside the class if they are necessary.

Follow-up
Rotate these roles every week so that different students are given the positions of responsibility.

NOTE: Young learners often really like having positions of responsibility in the class. It gives them a stake in what's going on and helps build self-esteem. By changing these on a regular and fair basis, you ensure that everyone takes part.

Class Helper Role Cards

The Timekeeper
Possible responsibilities:
- to announce when the class starts
- to announce when the class is over
- to tell the teacher what time it is when he / she asks
- to call time on timed activities.

The Boardkeeper
Possible responsibilities:
- to clean the board at the beginning of class
- to write the day and date on the board
- to clean the board at the end of class.

The Messenger
Possible responsibilities:
- to distribute worksheets or papers to students around the class
- to collect work in for the teacher
- to deliver any messages **outside** the classroom as necessary during the week.

The Attendance-taker
Possible responsibilities:
- to take attendance for the teacher at the beginning of class.

A Suitable Model

Level	From elementary onwards
Aim	To raise the self-esteem of disruptive students with feedback on written work
Duration	10 minutes
Materials	A few lines from any disruptive student's written work
Language / Skills	Varied

Preparation
Choose a piece of homework written by a disruptive student and correct a few lines.

Procedure
1 Collect homework or set a short written task in class in order to ensure that you have a sample of written work by a troublesome student who may not normally do any homework.

2 Correct any language mistakes in the student's text but make sure the meaning is still the same.

3 In the next lesson, tell the students they are going to have a dictation as feedback on the written text.

4 Tell them the text is something one of them has written and that you have corrected. Do not mention the name of the student who wrote the original extract.

5 Dictate the student's text as feedback to the whole class on the written task.

6 Ask the students to check their dictations in pairs.

7 Point out or elicit positive features of the text and recommend that the class bear these features in mind in their future work.

Variation
Thank the student in front of the class at the end of the task if you feel this will raise the student's self-esteem further.

A Quiet Word After Class

Level	Any
Aim	To provide positive feedback and raise the self-esteem of disruptive students
Duration	2 minutes after class
Materials	None
Language / Skills	Words of praise

Procedure
1 The next time one of the more troublesome students behaves well in class (by participating well with a group, speaking more in English than usual, completing the exercises on time, etc.), ask him / her discreetly to stay back after class for a moment.

2 When the other students have left the room, tell the student how pleased you were with his / her work today. For example:

I noticed you spoke a lot more English today, I thought that was really good.
I saw that you finished all your exercises today, well done.
I've noticed that your English is getting better, and I wanted to tell you.

NOTE: This works on the same principle as Catch Them Being Good on page 55, namely that 'bad' students are more accustomed to being asked to stay after class because they have misbehaved. This way you are giving extra reinforcement to the good behaviour.

Invisible Body

Level	Any
Aim	To calm the class after a noisy spell
Duration	15 minutes
Materials	Pencil and A4 paper
Language / Skills	Parts of the body: *head, hand, shin, chin, cheek, eyes*, etc.

Procedure

1 After a noisy spell or a disruptive incident, ask the students to take a piece of paper and a pencil.

2 Explain that you are going to read out some words that have to do with parts of the body (e.g. *head, hand*) and that they have to write down the words on their piece of blank paper roughly in the position they imagine they should be on an 'invisible body'.

3 Dictate the words, pausing to give students time to write them down.

4 After you have dictated a dozen or so words (depending on the time available and the level of the class), ask the students to check their work with a partner. They should check for spelling and content: do they have the parts of the body in the same position?

5 Conduct a brief feedback session with the whole class to make sure all the students have the correct words in the right place.

6 When the feedback session is over, ask the students to link their words to form an outline of a body. Ask them to compare bodies.

Variations

With young children, replace 'bodies' with 'monsters'. The monsters can be coloured in. The end-product can form the basis of a mini-exhibition on the walls of the classroom.

You could use the same procedure to work on the following:

- names of countries (write where they are on a world map)
- rooms (write where they are on a floor plan of a flat)
- classroom furniture (write where they are in the class).

Listen Carefully

Level	Any
Aims	To encourage students to be quiet and listen
Duration	10 minutes
Materials	Instructions on cards / slips of paper
Language / Skills	Listening; speaking

Preparation

Write out the instructions for Student As and Student Bs below and make enough copies for each student.

Student A

1 Think of something interesting to tell your partner. You could talk about:

    a film   a book   some gossip   a place   a hobby

2 Tell your partner about it with a lot of enthusiasm. You will have one minute. Keep talking.

Student B

Your partner is going to talk about something they think is very interesting. You show **no interest** in what they are saying. Show this by:

- your voice
- never making eye contact
- looking over their shoulder
- staring into space.

Procedure

1 Tell the students they are going to practise their listening and speaking skills.

2 Put the students in pairs and give each pair a copy of the instructions for Student A and Student B. Give them a minute to think about what they are going to talk about.

3 Ask them to do the activity. They speak for one minute.

4 Ask the pairs to reverse roles. Student A listens while Student B talks for one minute on a different topic. Explain that this time, Student A must:

- remain silent for one minute
- maintain eye contact
- give feedback only by nodding saying 'hmm'.

5 When the minute is up, Student A repeats as accurately as possible what Student B said, in the first person (this is to avoid this task becoming a task in reported speech!).

6 Ask the students to discuss the two experiments.

Mosaic Writing

Level	From elementary onwards
Aim	To provide practice in writing in a supportive atmosphere; to build a group dynamic where everyone participates
Duration	30 minutes
Materials	Pen and paper
Language / Skills	Varied

Procedure

1 Give the students a title of a composition. For example: *My Favourite School Subject*

2 Ask them to brainstorm ideas together in pairs under these headings:

Useful Vocabulary	Grammar / Tenses	Topics
History Maths boring useful	present simple future: *It will be useful*	school subjects the teacher jobs

3 Elicit some ideas from the whole class and ask one or two students to write up the ideas on the board, under the correct heading.

4 When there are enough ideas on the board, the students begin to write on one of the topics.

5 After a couple of minutes, say: *Stop! Circulate!*

6 The students pass on their composition to another person, who continues exactly where the previous writer left off.

7 After a minute or so, say: *Stop! Circulate!*

8 Continue until you have half a dozen exchanges. (It could be more if you have more time.)

9 When the composition is long enough, each student will have a different version of the topic, produced by half a dozen or more fellow-students.

10 At home, the students write their own version of the 'mosaic' composition.

Dream Game

Level	From intermediate onwards
Aim	To practise writing; to guide writing with questions; to personalise writing
Duration	30 minutes
Materials	Pen and paper
Language / Skills	Narrative tenses; adjectives to describe objects

Procedure

1 Tell the students that you want them to imagine that they're walking down a path, any path, anywhere. Ask them to describe the path in writing:
Is it straight / winding / narrow / wide?
Is it in a forest / mountain / beach / city?

2 Tell the students that as they are walking along the path, they find a stick on the ground. Ask them to describe the stick. They need to think about: size, age, colour, weight.

3 Ask them to write down what they do with the stick:
Do you pick it up / kick it / throw it away?

4 Next, they come across a fallen tree. Ask them to describe it. They need to think about: size, age, colour.

5 What do they do now?
Do you jump over / go round the tree?

6 Next, the students see a bear on the path. They describe the bear and what they do.

7 After this, they come to a river. They describe the river and what they do.

8 Finally, they come to a wall. The wall is too high to climb, too long to walk around and they cannot dig under it. What do they do?

9 Give them the solution below and ask them to go back and interpret their answers.

Solution
- The path represents your interpretation of life in general.
- The stick represents life's small problems and how you deal with them.
- The tree represents life's big problems and how you deal with them.
- The bear represents the opposite sex.
- The river represents marriage.
- The wall represents death.

'I Like' Dictation

Level	From elementary onwards
Aim	To provide practice in writing in a supportive atmosphere; to calm a noisy class down
Duration	30 minutes
Materials	Pen and paper; slips of paper
Language / Skills	Varied (here: likes / dislikes; *can* for ability)

Procedure

1 Hand out slips of paper and ask the students to write one sentence about themselves using *like / dislike* or *can*. Ask early finishers to write a second sentence. For example:

I like watermelon but I dislike carrots.
I can speak French; I can play tennis.

2 Go round the class, checking and making sure the students' sentences are correct.

3 Collect the completed slips.

4 Hand out sheets of paper and ask the students to write all the names of the students in the class down the left-hand margin, like this:

Maria
John
Peter

5 Redistribute a dozen or so of the slips to the class at random.

6 Ask the students with a slip to read out the sentences one by one, giving the rest of the class time to write them down. Allow the student reading to read out the sentence twice.

7 The class writes the information next to the student to whom they think it applies. If they don't know and can't guess the person, then they should write the information anyway, at the bottom of the page or on the back of the page.

8 When the dictation is complete, the students check in pairs for form (spelling, vocabulary, grammar) and for content (do they agree on the person?).

9 Do a whole-class feedback. How many people were right in their guesses?

NOTE: You can repeat the dictation on other days with the leftover slips of paper.

Collective Dictation

Level	From intermediate onwards
Aim	To raise students' self-esteem; to strengthen group cohesion
Duration	30 minutes
Materials	Pen and paper
Language / Skills	Listening and writing

Procedure

1 Divide the class into two groups.
Group 1 completes the following stem sentence on a slip of paper:

I like watching TV because ...

Group 2 completes the following stem sentence on a slip of paper:

I enjoy going to the cinema because ...

2 Collect the slips and take them home. Prepare two paragraphs based on the two sentences (see examples below):

- correct the errors
- connect the fragments into a whole
- bring the level of the text up to a higher standard by modifying the grammar and vocabulary
- supply any ideas which are needed to enrich the text and facilitate the task.

Example paragraphs based on students' own sentences
Paragraph 1
Children like watching TV for a number of reasons. First of all, there are a lot of sports programmes but there are also comedies and quiz shows. ...
Paragraph 2
Some people, however, prefer going to the cinema. The cinema is more exciting because of the large screen. ...

3 In the next class, dictate the two paragraphs.

4 The students read over their text individually and search the text to find their original sentence. They underline it.

5 They search the text again to find any connecting devices you have used in the new, connected version of the sentences.

6 Now ask them to compare their text with another student and to make sure their texts are the same.

Follow-up

The students write a third paragraph, using the two dictated paragraphs as their model.

I Remember ...

Level	From intermediate onwards
Aim	To get students to reflect on events from their past; to calm a noisy class down
Duration	30 minutes
Materials	Pen and Paper
Language / Skills	Listening, writing and speaking; *remember + -ing.*

Procedure

1 Ask the students to copy the following table:

Ages						
2–5	6–10	11–12	13–16	17–19	20–25	26–30

2 Tell them you are going to dictate things that happen to us at various ages. Examples you could use are:

losing teeth   falling in love
feeling cold   taking exams
feeling angry   feeling sad
feeling anxious   thinking about my hair
riding my bike   leaving home
needing money

3 Ask them to write the information under the appropriate column, depending on how old they were when they remember having this experience.

4 Start dictating sentences like these:
I remember losing a tooth …
I remember falling in love …

5 When the dictation is over, the students turn to a partner and use the completed table to talk to each other about their memories. They should give more specific details (why, when, where, etc.). For example:
I remember feeling anxious when I was sixteen years old; I had to take an important exam.

6 When they have finished chatting with one person, they should turn to someone else.

Follow-up

The students write a brief report on what they have learnt about their fellow students.

Catch Them Being Bad

Level	Any
Aim	To alert students' attention to violation of class rules
Duration	A few seconds
Materials	None
Language / Skills	Question forms; statements

Procedure

1 When students are breaking a written or unwritten rule while you are working with a student in another part of the room, ask the offender(s) in a firm voice:
(Name) what's going on over there? I'll be with you in a moment.
(Name) you're out of your seat.
(Name) you're talking loudly.
(Name) you're not working – what should you be doing now?

2 Ask the class to get into groups and recall and write down the class rules (see the activity on page 44). How many can they remember?

NOTE: Remember that 'what' questions are more effective than 'why' questions. They place the responsibility for feedback on the students themselves.

Catch Them Being Good

Level	Any
Aim	To provide positive feedback and raise the self-esteem of disruptive students
Duration	A few seconds
Materials	None
Language / Skills	None

Procedure

1 When you notice a usually disruptive student behaves well (e.g. by completing an exercise, or answering a question correctly), respond by praising the student publicly. Disruptive students are usually accustomed to being caught out for being bad.

2 Here are some examples of things you could say:
   That's exactly the answer I was waiting for!
   Excellent answer, well done!
   Well done! You've finished the exercise … in record time, too!
   Did everyone hear (name)? He / She had the right answer.
   Yes, you've got the right idea. Excellent.

NOTE: Make sure you do this for the well-behaved students as well and in equal measure (if possible!). Disruptive students tend to get more teacher attention anyway (even if for the wrong reasons), and this can be seen as unfair by the other students.

What Happened to the Class?

Level	Any
Aim	To 'refresh' a previously disruptive class by changing the classroom layout
Duration	Five minutes
Materials	None
Language / Skills	None

Preparation

You need a class with chairs / tables that can be moved around.

Procedure

1 Stop the class after a noisy activity. Explain that you would like to reorganise the seating.

2 Quickly sketch on the board how you would like the seating arrangement to be. Here are some possible seating arrangements:
   - a horseshoe shape – for whole-class discussion
   - rows – for 'serious' solo work, like writing or a dictation
   - small groupings of tables together – for group work
   - chairs facing each other – for speaking pairwork

3 Tell the students they have three minutes to make the class seating arrangement match the sketch on the board. Help out.

4 Continue the next part of the lesson.

Variations

Instead of changing the seating around, ask the students to sit on the front of their desks and continue the lesson that way.

Tell the students to stand in a semi-circle (no pens or paper in hand) and continue the class that way. This is good for drilling or other pronunciation work.

If it is not too cold, sit on the floor in a circle. This is good for refocusing the attention, for telling a story or for whole-group discussions.

Reorganise the class seating to something completely different **before** the students arrive. As they come in, direct them to their places.

NOTE: It is also a good idea for you to change the place from which **you** usually teach from time to time.

Be My Guest

Level	Any
Aim	To introduce an outside visitor to the class
Duration	20 to 30 minutes
Materials	None
Language / Skills	Question forms

Preparation

Find an English-speaking friend or family member who could come to your class for the last half an hour or so. Ask your guest beforehand to think of an interesting anecdote or experience about their life that they would be willing to share. This could be a great / terrible job they had, a brush with death, a meeting with a star.

Procedure

1 At the beginning of the lesson, explain briefly that someone is coming to meet the class for the last half hour, but don't make too much of this now.

2 Twenty minutes before your guest is due to arrive, tell the students to put away their books. Wait for silence.

3 Tell the students that very shortly the guest will come in. Tell them very briefly about the interesting experience / fact that the guest is going to share with them. For example:

Today's guest was once attacked by a shark. She is going to tell you about it, but you have to prepare some questions for her first.

4 Put the students in pairs and instruct them to write three to five questions they could ask.

5 Check some of the questions as a whole group. Make sure the students have different questions (not *What is your name?* thirty times!).

6 When they are ready, bring in the guest and invite the students to ask their questions, with the guest answering and asking questions, too.

Variations

If your guest has a great story, and even better, a photo to go with it, then show the photo around the class at the getting-ready stage.

If your guest is a non-native speaker of English, you could ask them to come in and talk about their experience of learning English and when they have used it in their lives.

Team Teaching

Level	Any
Aim	To introduce another teacher to the lesson
Duration	A full lesson or part of a lesson
Materials	None
Language / Skills	This will vary

Preparation

Find a colleague who will come and teach a class, or part of a class, with you and plan the class together. Ask them beforehand to plan the lesson with you. It need only be a part of a lesson, say, fifteen minutes. Decide who will do what – make the stages very clear (e.g. introduction, warm-up, presentation, practice).

Procedure

1 Start the lesson by introducing the other teacher to the students. Explain that today you will **both** be teaching the class.

2 Take turns teaching different parts of the class. Here are some possibilities:

- One teacher does the teacher-fronted part of the lesson and both teachers circulate and monitor the rest of the lesson.
- Both teachers take turns running different activities.
- The students form two groups and one teacher takes one group and the other teacher takes the other group. They swap groups halfway through the class.
- If there is a game-type activity, each teacher is responsible for a team.

NOTE: Make sure you return the favour to the other teacher!

3

Mixed-level Classes

'Help! I have a mixed ability class! How on earth can I teach?'

All classes are made up of mixed levels. As soon as you put two people together, you have a mixed-level situation, especially if mixed levels are seen as more than a question of ability as demonstrated in tests of language proficiency. Mixed-level classes are also, and amongst other things, the result of:

- the different learning styles of students
- the pace at which they each learn
- their level and kind of motivation
- their personal interests
- their background knowledge
- any social problems they may be facing.

Mixed-level teaching is thus only one problem (or challenge) faced by teachers and it cuts across other 'problems', such as failure to achieve results, discipline and – the number one factor in learning a language – motivation, or the lack of it. **How** we confront the problem of 'mixed ability' or, more accurately, 'mixed-level' teaching will make a big difference to the progress we make with our students. Because mixed-level teaching is defined by diversity and making the most of diversity in the classroom, it goes to the heart of teaching.

So, in practical terms, how do we deal with the mixed-level class?

Someone said there is nothing as practical as a good theory and the ideas of Lev Vygotsky are a great source of inspiration in building techniques for co-operative learning and making the most of diversity in the classroom. Some of these ideas have been set out in the box on page 59.

Derived from the principles outlined by Vygotsky, there are different ways of generating practical classroom techniques which we have adopted for the purposes of organising this chapter.

3.1 Different Level, Different Task

'The material is too hard for half the class, or it's too easy. It's almost like I need two coursebooks.'

The activities in the first section of this chapter suggest ways of setting different tasks for different students. This does not mean preparing two or more different lessons for the same class! Any solutions to meeting the diverse needs of students should involve a minimum amount of preparation and a maximum 'pay-off', not only in terms of language practice but also in terms of building key factors in motivating a class: self-esteem and rapport.

A basic principle will be to exploit, wherever possible, the same text but to vary the tasks students perform on that text. This principle can be applied to individual items of language or activities designed to practice the four skills: speaking, reading, writing and listening.

3.2 Extending Tasks

'The quick students finish early and then disrupt the class because they are bored.'

The activities in the second section of this chapter are flexible, personalised and open-ended. Not only are they mixed-ability friendly, they should help deal with the problem of early finishers.

The early finisher is already on the road to becoming a discipline problem. The slow student never finishes any activity and gets demoralised. It is therefore imperative to take the early finisher into account when we deal with the difficulty of mixed-level teaching, while at the same time allowing the slower ones the satisfaction of completing a task successfully.

3.3 Catering for Learner Styles

'The other day we did an activity, and Marta (who is usually the slowest) responded really well! I had no idea, and it has made me see her differently.'

In this section, we recognise that different people learn things in different ways. We have chosen three dominant learner styles to illustrate how you can introduce a variety of activities, thereby 'casting the net' wider.

Visual
Visual activities cater for those who like to learn by **seeing** the subject matter – pictures, diagrams, words written on the board, video and visualisation activities.

Auditory
Auditory activities cater for those learners who need to learn by **listening** – lectures, rhymes, talking to each other and music.

Kinaesthetic
Kinaesthetic activities cater for those learners who like to learn by physically **doing things** – using mime, gesturing to demonstrate ideas, making use of physical movement in the classroom.

Of course, you can draw simultaneously on more than one of these styles (sometimes referred to as VAK) for the benefit of the individual learner and the group. The more the merrier, as that way you are more likely to appeal to the diversity in the class.

3.4 One Teacher, One Class

'There's more to mixed-level teaching than just adding different kinds of exercise for different kinds of student; indeed, this approach may exacerbate the tensions in the class rather than reduce them.'

The tips and techniques in this section help to address the challenge of keeping the class together.

One way of solving a mixed-ability class is to subdivide it into smaller and smaller groups, assigning each group its own teacher. Ultimately, coming back to what we said earlier, this means you would need one teacher for every student. In practice, this is simply impossible and assumes the students are learning in isolation from each other.

The truth is that there is (usually) one teacher and one class. And our job is to keep the class together. The activities in earlier sections can help us achieve this, but in the long run we need to develop ways of adjusting our everyday teaching to meet the challenge. This includes thinking about how we nominate students, how we group them and how we correct them in class. It means building on diversity, not banging our heads against it.

3.5 One Class, Not Several

'I feel as if there are two groups in the class – the bright ones and the slow ones.'

A teaching approach which highlights the differences in ability and achievement is likely to make this tendency in many mixed-level classes worse rather than better. The students themselves know about the differences in ability and get impatient with each other, so there is an inherent danger of the class breaking up right from the very start. The best way to improve this situation is to come up with activities and adaptations of existing material which unify rather than divide.

There are a number of ways of building on the group's sense of unity:

- making tasks flexible enough to accommodate different learning styles
- drawing on learner input and personalising tasks
- encouraging co-operation and peer questioning
- using activities that do not necessarily have a linguistic outcome but reinforce rapport.

Strategies such as these build on the principle of collaboration by drawing on individual strengths, however relative those strengths may be, as students contribute to the task according to their current abilities and interests.

To sum up, in this chapter the following principles have been applied:

- Students support each other.
- The teacher supports the students.
- Tasks are co-constructed.
- Tasks are flexible.
- Tasks are open-ended.
- Tasks are 'intelligently' varied.
- Students work on their own material.
- The material is of an appropriate level.
- The material is of interest to the learners.
- Learner input is culture sensitive.
- The learner's mother tongue is a resource.
- Error is a source of learner strength and growth.
- Self-esteem is raised.
- Positive attitudes are encouraged.
- Rapport and group dynamics are strengthened.

How we deal with the 'difficulty' of mixed-level teaching will be a reflection of our very beliefs about teaching and learning. Above all, how we tackle the diverse needs of our learners depends on whether we really believe in their potential or not. Remember the students who said about their best teacher: *She believed in me and made me believe in myself* or *She wanted us all to succeed, not only the good ones.*

The Zone of Proximal Development

Lev Vygotsky defines the Zone of Proximal Development (ZPD) as the 'distance between the actual development (of the learner) and the level of potential development as determined through problem solving under adult guidance or in collaboration with more capable peers'. (Vygotsky, 1978:86)

What learners can do with the assistance of others is more indicative of their mental development than what they can do alone. Thus, the ZDP defines those mental skills that have not yet matured ('the buds') but are in the process of maturation ('the flowers').

Scaffolding is one of the many forms taken by the specific means of assistance provided by the more able members in the ZPD, in which more capable members of the class share responsibility with the 'less capable' members in the completion of tasks. The teacher gradually lets the 'less capable' students assume greater responsibility for the activities.

Training is when the more expert members coach or directly instruct the learners in the completion of the task. What is jointly constructed eventually, through use in social contexts, becomes part of the individual's internalised knowledge.

Mediational means are tools which the more expert use to assist 'less capable' participants in noticing, ordering and remembering their involvement in communicative activities. Mediational means can be verbal, visual or physical. An example of mediational means is the 'leading question': in this strategy, the teacher offers leading questions to help the child solve a problem or complete a task.

Vygotsky's ZDP is a very useful framework for developing practical approaches to the challenges of mixed-level classes as it gives all the learners a role to play in a mutually supportive and collaborative environment.

Complementary Gap-fills

Level	Any
Aim	To vary the level of difficulty of gap-fill exercises
Duration	Variable
Materials	A coursebook gap-fill
Language / Skills	Varied

Preparation

Prepare two worksheet adaptations of a gap-fill activity from your course materials. For the first one, have fewer gaps and choose easier items. Make the second one more difficult, with more gaps of more difficult items. Make sure you make as many copies as you think you will need, especially if you are going to allow the students to choose which task they do.

Procedure

1 Put the students into 'mixed' pairs, based on your knowledge of their relative strengths. This will facilitate the 'stronger' student helping the less advanced.

2 Produce your two versions of the gap-fill text: A and B.

Task A (less challenging)
Six gaps and 'easier' items

Task B (more challenging)
Ten gaps and more difficult items

3 Explain to the students that there are two versions of the task: A and B. One is easier, the other more difficult. Ask the students to put their hands up if they wish to choose A or B and give out the appropriate tasks.

4 The students complete their version of the gap-fill text.

5 They feed back to each other, comparing their answers if they chose the same task or getting feedback from their partner if they chose a different task.

6 Conduct whole-class feedback for both tasks.

Variations

The text used may be based on a song, in which case the students can round off the checking of their answers by listening to the song.

Early finishers can have a go at the task they didn't choose. If you have time and energy, prepare a third version of the task, by providing 15 gaps (much more difficult) or only four gaps (much easier).

NOTE: This simple task demonstrates the possibilities of working at two or three levels with an activity.

Complementary Tasks

Level	Any
Aim	To facilitate the co-operative reading of a text
Duration	Variable (depending on text and questions)
Materials	A coursebook reading text
Language / Skills	Varied

Preparation

Prepare a worksheet adaptation of the coursebook comprehension questions (see Task B, below). Prepare to write the extra version of the task on the board. If you prefer, you can make copies of the adaptation, making sure you have as many copies as you think you will need.

Procedure

1 Put the students into 'mixed' pairs, based on your knowledge of their relative strengths. This will facilitate the 'stronger' student helping the less advanced.

2 The students read the text from the book, for example on the topic of a penpal advert.

3 Explain that there are two tasks that go with this text: the one in the coursebook and the one on the board. They can choose A (less challenging) or B (more challenging).

Task A (less challenging)
The student As open their coursebooks and write the answers to these questions:

1 *How many of the people are 13 years old?*
2 *How many boys are there?*
3 *Who doesn't eat meat?*
4 *Who likes football?*
5 *Who lives in the country?*

Task B (more challenging)
The student Bs write the questions for these answers on a worksheet:

1 *There are three.*
2 *There are four.*
3 *Elena doesn't.*
4 *James does.*
5 *Chris does.*

In pairs, the students compare their answers.

4 Do some whole-class feedback.

Acknowledgement: Bowler and Parminter, English Teaching *professional* Issue 13.

Dual Choice, Multiple Choice

Level	From intermediate onwards
Aim	To vary the difficulty of reading comprehension exercises
Duration	Variable
Materials	A coursebook multiple-choice reading comprehension
Language / Skills	Varied

Preparation

Prepare two or three worksheet adaptations of a multiple-choice reading comprehension. Make sure you make as many copies as you think you will need. Blank out one or more distractors (see Note below) in the new versions of the task.

Procedure

1 Explain that the students are going to do a multiple-choice reading at three levels of difficulty: A, B or C (ranging from less challenging to very challenging). They can choose which level they wish to work at.

2 Hand out your multiple-choice reading text, according to the ones chosen by the students. The example below follows a reading text on the subject of Melina's trip to the cinema.

Task A (less challenging)
To make the text easier, **one** of the three or four distractors has been removed.
> *Melina didn't enjoy the film because:*
> **A** *she was tired.*
> **B** *she'd seen it before.*
> **C** *it was too long.*

Task B (more challenging)
This is the original question, with the correct option and **all** the distractors, as it appears in the book.
> *Melina didn't enjoy the film because:*
> **A** *she was tired.*
> **B** *she'd seen it before.*
> **C** *it was too long.*
> **D** *it was too violent.*

Task C (most challenging)
The correct option and all the distractors have been blanked out.
> *Melina didn't enjoy the film because* _____.

NOTE: Multiple-choice tests usually have three or four options (A, B, C or D) of which one is the correct answer and the others are 'distractors'. The more 'distractors' there are, the more difficult the task.

More Support, Less Support

Level	Any
Aim	To vary the difficulty of reading comprehension exercises
Duration	Variable
Materials	A coursebook reading comprehension; slips of paper with instructions
Language / Skills	Varied

Preparation

Take a comprehension text from the coursebook and produce two versions of the comprehension questions on pieces of paper: one carrying extra support for the weaker students.

Procedure

1 Explain that you have two sets of instructions for the same task: one easier (A) and one more difficult (B). The students have to choose which level they would like to work at.

2 Give the slips out to the students according to the level they choose.

Task A (less challenging)
> *Answer the questions in the book. Here are the answers mixed up.*

Task B (more challenging)
> *Answer the questions in the book.*

3 Organise some feedback with the whole class or in pairs.

Split the Questions

Level	Any
Aim	To provide comprehension questions for students of different levels
Duration	20 minutes
Materials	A coursebook reading comprehension
Language / Skills	Reading

Preparation

Take any reading comprehension text which includes about ten questions. If there are fewer, add a couple of questions of your own to make a larger number. Rewrite the comprehension questions as two lists: A and B. For the A list, include easier 'information retrieval' questions – that is, questions for which the answer should be relatively easy to pick out from the text. For the B list, include questions that are more difficult or that require more interpretation of the text. For example:

List A (less challenging)
1 *Where did Romeo and Juliet meet?*
2 *What is Juliet's second name?*
3 *What is Romeo's surname?*
4 *Where do they decide to meet tomorrow?*

List B (more challenging)
1 *What is the problem between the two families?*
2 *How does Romeo talk?*
3 *Why is Juliet afraid?*
4 *What does her father say?*

Procedure

1 Ask the students to work in pairs: one A and one B. Give them the copies of their questions. Explain that they should only answer their own questions.

2 After five to ten minutes, ask the students to swap information to complete all ten questions.

3 Get whole-class feedback.

Variation

A simpler way of using questions in the book without making new lists is to just divide students into 'odd' and 'even': students answer only the odd or even questions in the coursebook and then exchange answers. The disadvantage, of course, is that in this way you cannot divide the questions into 'easier' and 'more difficult'.

Gap Listening, Choice Listening

Level	Any
Aim	To provide more or less support for listening practice
Duration	Variable (depending on text and questions)
Materials	A song or listening passage from the coursebook
Skills / Language	Listening for detail

Preparation

Choose a listening text or a song from your coursebook and prepare two sets of questions for it. For example:

Task A (less challenging)
Instead of gaps, give two choices:
Jane wants to take the bus / train to New York.

Task B (more challenging)
There are gaps for the students to complete:
Jane wants to take the _____ to New York.

Make as many copies as you think you will need.

Procedure

1 Play the listening once with books closed.

2 Distribute the questions. Give the stronger students the questions with gaps and the weaker students the questions with a choice.

3 Play the listening again.

4 Ask if anyone needs to hear it a third time. If several of them do, play it a third time.

5 Pair up weaker and stronger students to compare their answers.

6 Go through the answers as a class, making sure you alternate between asking a stronger student and a weaker student for the answers.

Books Open, Books Closed

Level	Any
Aim	To make a listening comprehension task more challenging for stronger students
Duration	Variable (depending on text and questions)
Materials	A listening exercise from the coursebook
Skills / Language	Listening for detail

Procedure

1 The next time you come to a listening comprehension in the coursebook, explain that there are two possibilities: more or less challenging. Ask the students to choose an option (you might want to encourage the stronger students to do the more challenging option).

2 Give the following instructions:

Task A (less challenging)
Open your books on page 00. Do comprehension exercise X.

Task B (more challenging)
Keep your books closed. After the listening, write down five key facts that are important for the comprehension of the text.

3 Play the listening once and let the students work on their tasks.

4 Play the listening again so that they can check their answers and add anything they think they have missed.

5 Put the students into pairs and tell them to compare answers.

Complete the Story

Level	From intermediate onwards
Aim	To provide listening practice at different levels
Duration	20 minutes
Materials	A short story (200–300 words)
Language / Skills	Narrative tenses

Preparation

Choose a story to read in class and prepare stem sentences in lists of three levels of difficulty. This example is based on the well-known story of *The Pied Piper*:

Task A (less challenging)
1 *The town was full of ...*
2 *The people were very ...*
3 *The stranger was playing a ...*

Task B (more challenging)
1 *There were too many ...*
2 *The mayor said ...*
3 *The stranger spoke ...*

Task C (most challenging)
1 *The people complained that ...*
2 *As they were speaking, ...*
3 *The stranger offered to ...*

Make as many copies as you will need.

Procedure

1 Give the students three lists of stem sentences to complete while they listen to the story. Tell them they can choose stems from list A (less difficult), B (more difficult) or C (most difficult).

2 Read or tell the story. After the first reading, the students try to answer their questions.

3 Read the story again. This time, the students can answer more questions from the same category or they can switch to another one (this is designed to provide a greater challenge for students whatever their level).

Jigsaw Pictures

Level	Any
Aim	To develop listening skills; to activate visual intelligence
Duration	20 minutes
Materials	A picture; pencil and paper
Language / Skills	Prepositions of place

Preparation

Find a suitable picture for the level of the class (preferably a line drawing).

Make two photocopies of the picture that you intend use in this describe-and-draw activity.

Blank out certain details from each picture, erasing more details from one picture than the other (see examples opposite).

Make as many photocopies of each version as you think you will need.

Procedure

1 Give each student one of the two versions of the picture according to their perceived ability.

Task A (less challenging)
The students get the picture with fewer details blanked out.

Task B (more challenging)
The students get the picture with the greater number of blanks.

2 Choose a 'good' student to describe the original picture (no details blanked out). You should intervene only in case of miscommunication between the 'describer' and the class.

3 The students then work in pairs (As and Bs) to compare their versions of the picture and exchange visual details in order to help each other complete any missing parts.

NOTE: The use of visuals, alongside verbal tasks, will help reach a greater number of students in mixed-level classes. There are several more 'visual' activities later on in this chapter.

Original Picture

Task A Picture

Task B Picture

Truth or Lie?

Level	Any
Aim	To provide oral fluency practice at different levels of difficulty
Duration	10 minutes
Materials	A speaking activity from the coursebook
Skills / Language	Speaking; question practice

Preparation

Select a speaking activity from the coursebook that involves personal questions and answers. For example:

What do you do in your free time?
Do you have a hobby?
What do you like doing at the weekend?

Procedure

1 Set the students to work in pairs and ask and answer the questions in the usual way.

2 Tell them to work with a new partner.

3 Explain that they should repeat the activity, but when answering they can choose one of the following options:

Task A (less challenging)
Students answer the questions normally, just like the first time.

Task B (more challenging)
Students answer the questions all untruthfully, that is, they answer with a lie for each question.

4 When the students have finished the second round, tell them to work with a new partner. Add the following option:

Task C (most challenging)
Students answer the questions but, this time, as if they were a famous person. They have to tell their partner who they are first!

5 Instruct the students to choose one of the three options and repeat the activity a last time. Stress that it doesn't matter if they repeat the same option.

Mixed Ability, Mixed-up Sentences

Level	Any
Aim	To revise grammar structures
Duration	Variable (depending on text and questions)
Materials	A unit from the coursebook
Skills / Language	Word order

Procedure

1 Towards the end of a unit of the coursebook, tell the students to go back through the unit and pick out six to ten sentences from the grammar practice and copy them into their notebooks.

2 Tell them that they can choose the level at which they would like to do this activity: A (less challenging), B (more challenging) or C (most challenging).

3 Put them into pairs and instruct them to tell each other what level they have chosen.

4 Give the instructions for the exercise. Each student must take a sentence and rewrite it with the words in a different order, with the following options:

Task A (less challenging)
Write the first and last word of the sentence in the correct place, but mix up the order of the other words.

Task B (more challenging)
Write all the words in a different order.

Task C (most challenging)
Write the words in a different order and put in an extra word (e.g. *to, for, that, a*).

To show what you mean, do the following example with *What are you going to do?*

> **Task A:** *What going to you are do?* (Here *What* and *do* are in their correct positions.)
> **Task B:** *you do going what to are?* (Here the words are all jumbled.)
> **Task C:** *going do you for to what are?* (Here *for* is the extra word.)

5 When they are ready, tell the students to exchange papers with their partners. They rewrite the words in the correct order to make sentences.

6 When they finish, tell them to check their answers in pairs.

Choose Two ...

Level	Any
Aim	To extend a speaking activity
Duration	10 minutes
Materials	A coursebook speaking activity with several discussion questions
Skills / Language	Speaking

Procedure

1 The next time you come to a speaking activity which involves students asking each other several questions (more than four), ask them to read the questions silently.

2 Tell them to choose **two** of the questions they would like to ask a partner.

3 Put the students in pairs of a similar ability and let them ask their questions.

Early Finishers

The early finishers can ask each other the other questions in the speaking activity.

NOTE: The early finishers will often go on and do all the others regardless of whether you ask them to or not.

Repeat, Please!

Level	Any
Aim	To change speaking tasks so that they can be repeated
Duration	10 minutes
Materials	A coursebook speaking activity that students do in pairs or groups
Skills / Language	Speaking

Procedure

Assign the speaking activity in the coursebook as you normally would. Put the students in pairs of a similar ability.

Early Finishers

Tell the early finishers to repeat the task in one of the following ways:

- Ask the questions again, but this time giving answers that are completely untrue.
- Ask the questions again, but this time make it into a roleplay, with one student taking the role of someone else (see box for suggestions).
- Ask the questions again, but with a new partner. (For this, you need two pairs of early finishers.)

Sample Roles for Repeating Speaking Tasks

Answer the questions again, but this time answer in the 'role':

- the President of the United States
- the President of your country
- a film or music star (you choose)
- another person from your family
- the teacher
- another role (you choose).

The 'Early Finisher' Table

Level	Any
Aim	To keep a speaking class busy
Duration	Variable
Materials	Pictures plus questions from an old coursebook
Skills / Language	Speaking

Preparation
Take an old coursebook at the same level as one you are teaching. Cut out any speaking tasks in the book which are accompanied by questions. You should end up with a colourful array of pictures and questions.

Procedure
1 Display your pictures on a table at the front of the class.

2 Ask the students, in pairs or groups, to do the speaking task as assigned in their coursebook as you normally would.

Early Finishers
When they have completed the speaking task in the book, the early finishers come to the front and choose a picture-plus-questions to discuss in their pairs or groups. If they finish that one, they take another, and so on.

Variations
Having the pictures displayed on a table somewhere in the room adds 'colour' to the class but you may put the pictures-plus-questions in separate envelopes. Early finishers take an envelope and open it to find the task inside. There is an element of surprise – and fun – in this version.

You can recycle other sections of old coursebooks: grammar and vocabulary exercises and even short reading tasks.

You can mix the tasks to accommodate your students' preferred learning styles. On the 'early finisher table' you may leave speaking tasks (as above) but also grammar and vocabulary exercises and allow the early finishers to choose the kind of tasks they wish to focus on.

NOTE: Remember to collect in all the tasks borrowed by the early finishers so you can reuse them in future classes. You may wish to laminate the tasks to protect them from wear and tear.

Give Them the Slip

Level	Any
Aim	To maintain speaking momentum
Duration	10 minutes
Materials	A coursebook speaking activity with pictures that students do in pairs; slips of paper
Skills / Language	Speaking

Procedure
1 Ask the students to brainstorm questions they would ask about the pictures they have been given (in the book). The questions can be directly about the pictures or about topics suggested by the pictures.

2 In pairs, they write their questions on slips of paper, one slip per question. They should also write their name on the slip.

3 Collect in the slips and assign the speaking activity in the coursebook as you normally would.

Early Finishers
Give the early finishers a slip of paper with one of the questions written by the class. They discuss the question. If they finish the first 'extra' question, give them another one from your collection of slips.

Variation
You can also use the questions for a revision activity. Write a series of the questions (not the students' names) on the board and ask the students to decide which ones are well-formed questions and which are incorrect. They correct the incorrect ones.

NOTE: Learner-generated questions are more interesting for students than teachers' questions. There is a greater element of surprise and suspense (*What question am I going to get?* and *Who wrote it?*).

Too Many Questions

Level	Any
Aim	To develop reading skills; to keep early finishers busy
Duration	5 minutes
Materials	A reading comprehension with *yes / no* and *wh-* questions; slips of paper
Language / Skills	Reading

Procedure

1 In cases where there are six questions or more accompanying a reading comprehension task, ask the students, in pairs, to answer only three or four questions or only the odd questions (1, 3, 5) or even questions (2, 4, 6).

Early Finishers

Ask the early finishers to answer the other questions.

2 When the pairs are ready, they compare their answers.

Variations

Ask the students to choose the three or four questions they find easier / more interesting.

Write the topic of the reading comprehension on the board and ask the students to write on a slip of paper three questions they would like the text to answer. For example, if the text is about 'the most popular tourist destinations around the world' students may wish to know: 'which city has the most visitors?' or 'which city is most popular with young people?' and so on. Early finishers answer their own questions or those written by another pair.

Class Mascot

Level	Any
Aim	To extend vocabulary development; to provide an extra task
Duration	5 minutes
Materials	Some kind of class mascot; coursebook grammar or vocabulary exercises
Skills / Language	Writing

Preparation

At the beginning of the course, decide on a class mascot. See the Notes below.

Procedure

Set the grammar or vocabulary in the coursebook as you normally would.

Early Finishers

Tell the early finishers to write a sentence or two with the target grammar or vocabulary but linking it to the class mascot.

NOTES: This obviously works better with younger students, but it can also work with older learners too. In a Spanish class Lindsay once saw there was a little souvenir Mexican man on the shelf. The students called him José and made lots of sentences about him. At the end of the year he had quite a history!

A mascot is an animal, person or object that is thought to be lucky and that is used as a symbol for a team or organisation. Different kinds of class mascots could be:

- a drawing of a cartoon character
- a photograph of a famous person
- a puppet
- a stuffed toy animal
- an unusual object which you give a name to.

Questionnaire, Version 2

Level	Any
Aim	To suggest another angle on a questionnaire
Duration	10 minutes
Materials	A coursebook questionnaire
Language / Skills	Writing and speaking

Procedure

1 Assign a speaking questionnaire from your coursebook as you normally would.

2 Put the students into pairs of similar ability to do it.

Early Finishers

Ask pairs who finish early to make a similar questionnaire, but with a different focus. Here are some examples of how you could do this with different questionnaires.

Routines (practising the present tense):
How often do you watch TV?
Change the questions so they are in the past tense:
How often did you watch TV when you were a child?

Sports (practising sports vocabulary):
Did you play sports at school?
What sports did you like?
Change the questions so they are about food:
Did you eat at the school canteen?
What food did they serve at school?

Personal information (practising question forms):
Do you have a job?
Where do you work?
Change the questions so they are about a different person:
Does your mother / father have a job?
Where does she / he work?

3 While the early finishers are working on their new questionnaire, allow the others to finish.

4 When the others have finished, ask each pair to work with a pair of early finishers.

5 The early finishers interview the others with their new questions.

Deconstructing Words

Level	From elementary onwards
Aim	To extend vocabulary; to practise spelling
Duration	5 minutes
Materials	Dictionaries (optional)
Skills / Language	Spelling; vocabulary extension

Procedure

1 At the beginning of the lesson, choose a word that is in some way connected to the lesson. The longer the word, the better. For example, if you are doing a lesson on people from different countries, you could choose the word *nationality*.

2 Write your word on the board in the corner.

3 Begin your lesson as you normally would.

Early Finishers

Explain that during the lesson, if someone finishes a task early they should try to write as many new words from the letters of the word on the board into their notebooks. For example, *nationality* could give the following words:

nation	national
nil	tan
tin	tiny
not	latin
Italy	nail
tail	

If you have a dictionary, give it to the early finishers to check words they may be unsure of.

4 In the last five minutes of class, ask all the students to look at the word on the board and see if they can make any new words from it. Give them a minute or so, then elicit answers (the early finishers may have found more words, but this includes the students who hadn't finished early).

The Word Collection

Level	Any
Aim	To extend vocabulary development; to provide an extra task
Duration	5 minutes
Materials	A coursebook reading comprehension; dictionaries
Skills / Language	Reading; dictionary work

Procedure

1 Set the reading comprehension task in the coursebook as you normally would.

Early Finishers

Tell the early finishers to choose three words from the text and write them on a piece of paper along with the dictionary definition / translation.

2 When everyone has finished, collect the new words from the early finishers.

3 Go through the new words with the class as a follow-up: read out the translation or definition and ask the students to find the word in the text.

Variations

Ask the students to do this for two **new** words and two **familiar** words in the text. Repeat the same procedure, but asking the weaker students in the class to provide the familiar words in the last stage.

Once you have collected the words, make the last stage into a quiz between teams. Read out a definition or translation of the new word. The teams must consult and then write the original English word. Organise the teams so that there is a mixture of stronger and weaker students.

If you have space in the class, you could have a 'New Words' board where you write up and keep these new words and definitions / translations.

NOTE: You can also keep the definitions or translations in a box for future use: for recycling or testing. See The Testing Box, opposite.

The Testing Box

Level	Any
Aim	To involve early finishers in preparing revision questions
Duration	5 minutes
Materials	Index cards or small squares of paper; an empty shoebox
Skills / Language	Varied

Procedure

During the lesson, have a series of index cards or small pieces of notepaper available.

Early Finishers

When the students finish early, distribute two or three slips of paper and tell them choose two or three sentences from a grammar exercise in the unit.

On each slip they should write the exercise **question** on one side and the **answer** on the other. Check that the answer is correct before you put it in the testing box.

Follow-up

You can use this box of questions for quizzes or to include in tests.

Once you have several cards in the box, the early finishers could work together and test each other, pulling a question from the box and 'testing' the other person with it.

Proofreading

Level	Any
Aim	To involve early finishers in proofreading each other's work
Duration	5 minutes
Materials	A coursebook exercise
Skills / Language	Writing; editing

Procedure

Assign a writing activity from your coursebook as you normally would.

Early Finishers

When the students finish early, get them to proofread each other's work. Tell them to look out for spelling, punctuation or grammar mistakes and to <u>underline</u> these with a pencil. Tell them that they are not **correcting** the mistakes but **identifying** them.

When they have finished, tell them to return the exercise to its owner to check it again and make any corrections.

Variation

You could give the proofreaders a very simple 'correction code' like this to work with:

Correction Code	
WW	wrong word
X	word missing
‿‿‿	problem with word order
T	problem with verb tense
Sp	spelling mistake
P	punctuation
?	I don't understand this

NOTE: There are more suggestions on how you can code corrections yourself on page 105. Here you are giving the students a very simplified code to work with themselves.

Help!

Level	Any
Aim	To make use of early finishers to do feedback
Duration	5 minutes
Materials	A coursebook grammar or vocabulary exercise
Skills / Language	Varied

Procedure

1 Assign a grammar or vocabulary exercise as you normally would.

Early Finishers

If students finish early, discreetly approach them and check their work. Indicate which answers are good and which they need to change.

Ask them to prepare to present their answers to other students. They may think of explanations and further examples to make the point of the grammar or vocabulary exercise clearer.

2 When the other students have finished the exercise, put all the students into groups. There should be one early finisher in each group.

3 Tell the groups to go through and check their answers together.

4 The early finishers should feed back on the answers in each group and settle any questions where there is a difference of opinion.

5 Make sure, in whole-class feedback, that everyone now has the correct answers and understands why the answers are correct.

Variation

Once you have determined that the early finishers' work is correct, ask them to help one of their classmates who is having trouble with the exercise.

Timelines

Level	Any
Aim	To cater for visual learning styles; to raise awareness of past tenses
Duration	3–4 minutes
Materials	None
Language / Skills	Illustrating a verb tense

Procedure

1 When you come across a new tense in your coursebook (or revisit a tense), explain to your students that you are going to illustrate this tense with a diagram.

2 Draw the following on the board and explain that the vertical line represents 'now'.

3 Take a pen or chalk of a different colour and draw a line representing the tense on the chart. Write a sample sentence to illustrate the tense underneath the diagram. For example:

Present Continuous

She's working in the garden.

In this case, the broken line represents an action that began in the past, is ongoing now and continues to the future. The fact that it's broken means the action is *in progress*.

Examples of Timelines

Present Simple for 'always true' or facts

We live in France.

Past Continuous

It was raining that night.

Present Perfect for experiences

I've seen The Lord of the Rings *three times.*

Present Perfect for 'up to now'

1970s

Luke's taught English since the 1970s.

Variations

If your students are already familiar with timelines, you could give an example sentence, draw a partial timeline and ask them to complete it.

At higher levels, ask the students to draw their own visual representation of a given tense or combination of tenses in a sentence.

Draw and Explain

Level	From elementary onwards
Aim	Visual learning styles; to help support a speaking activity
Duration	5 minutes
Materials	Pen and paper
Skills / Language	Speaking; 'house' vocabulary

Procedure

1 Review (or teach) house vocabulary with the class: *living room*, *bedroom*, *kitchen*, etc.

2 Ask the students to take a piece of paper (or a blank page in their notebooks) and draw a floor plan of where they live. Tell them they can be as detailed as they like, but they must not label anything.

3 While they are doing this, draw a simple floor plan of your own house on the board.

4 Put the students into pairs: A and B. Give the following instructions:
> A, you explain your map to B.
> B, you listen. As A explains, you label A's map with English words.

5 Demonstrate the activity with a stronger student. Ask the student to come to the board. Explain which room is which, signalling for the student to label the rooms as you speak. Do this for a couple of rooms.

6 Tell the students to do the same in pairs.

Variations

You can use this same activity format with other things that students can represent easily with maps. For example:

- an ideal classroom
- your neighbourhood
- a place you visited
- a shopping centre you know.

Spidergrams

Level	Any
Aim	Visual learning styles; to teach vocabulary
Duration	2 minutes
Materials	None
Skills / Language	Lexical sets

Procedure

1 The next time you come across a lexical set in your coursebook, draw it on the board in the following manner, with the category in the middle of the diagram. The following is an example for the category *computer*:

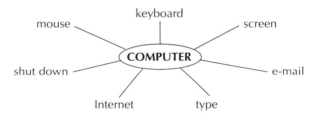

2 Elicit more words from the students and write them on the diagram.

3 Once the diagram is finished, tell the students to copy it into their notebooks.

Variation

This diagram can be as simple or complicated as you wish. You can have subcategories as well, which begin new diagrams.

NOTE: Don't feel you need to be restricted to circles – any shape will do. In fact, it is probably a good idea to vary the shape on the different occasions you do this activity.

In the Mind's Eye

Level	From elementary onwards
Aim	Visual learning styles; to introduce a topic
Duration	5 minutes
Materials	None (optional music)
Skills / Language	Listening and speaking

Preparation
Prepare a series of questions for a visualisation based on a coursebook topic and some music that 'goes' with the theme.

Procedure
1 At the beginning of the lesson, tell the students you would like them to put away their books and relax. Tell them that they can put their heads down if they like, or close their eyes. But they must be very quiet and listen to your questions.

2 Give the following instructions (these are based on the theme of food). If you have quiet music to accompany this, play it now.
> *Imagine it is a special day.* [pause] *You are very happy this day, because you are going to eat your favourite food.* [pause] *Imagine you are sitting at the table, and the food is going to arrive.* [pause] *Where are you? At home? At a restaurant? Imagine the place.* [pause] *Who are you with? Imagine the other people in the room.* [pause] *What can you smell? Imagine the smells in the room.* [pause] *Just at this moment, the food arrives …*

3 Tell the students to open their eyes (or lift their heads up). They should turn to a partner and explain what they visualised. To help them remember, write the following on the board:
> *What day?*
> *Where?*
> *Who with?*
> *What smell?*

4 When the students have told each other about the food they were thinking of, do some whole-class feedback, asking individual students to report on what their partners said.

5 Begin your lesson from the book in the usual way.

Artists and Dictators

Level	From intermediate onwards
Aim	Visual learning styles; to develop listening skills
Duration	15 minutes
Materials	A picture; pencil and paper
Language / Skills	Prepositions of place

Preparation
Find a suitable picture for the class level to bring with you to the lesson. For example, a line-drawing of parts of the body or parts of a house. There are many of these in coursebooks and dictionaries.

Label the picture with any items of vocabulary which you think the student-describer may not know (see below) and add any other useful expressions.

Procedure
1 Give one of your 'good' students the picture you have chosen and ask them to describe the picture to the rest of the class. They must not show the picture to the class.

2 The rest of the students listen and draw.

3 At the end of the 'student dictation', the students compare their pictures in pairs or small groups and help each other to complete any missing parts or correct any misunderstandings.

4 To check their answers, ask another 'good' student to describe the picture again. If the second student introduces new details, the students adjust their pictures accordingly.

Variations
A 'weaker' student can be given the role of dictator-describer if the labelling of the picture is more detailed and thereby easier to describe than to draw.

The task can be made easier and more fun by having the student-dictator flash the picture to the class very quickly and so giving them a partial impression of what is in the picture. Then the dictation begins.

Choose Your Words, Draw Your Picture

Level	From elementary onwards
Aim	Visual learning styles; to revise vocabulary
Duration	15 minutes
Materials	Pencil and paper
Language / Skills	Varied

Procedure

1 Elicit from the students the kind of things they might see in particular settings. For example: *a field, a living room, a classroom.*

2 Ask students of different levels to come to the board and write items of vocabulary related to a particular topic of a visual nature.

3 Ask more students to come to the board and add words and phrases till the board contains about twenty lexical items. For example, if the topic is 'a field', you will end up with something like this:

> tree   river   cow   hill   bush   farmer
> gate   fence   sun   clouds   rain

4 The students draw a picture to include any of the items in the vocabulary list.

5 Erase the words from the board.

6 Ask the students to compare their pictures and identify the items that have been drawn.

Follow-up
Students can be asked to write a description of their picture.

NOTE: This activity allows students to work at their own level but it also gives the 'weaker' ones an opportunity to construct a high level of lexis by drawing on the knowledge of other members of the class.

Variation
Ask the students, in pairs, to describe their picture to their partner, who draws it.

Variations on Reading Aloud

Level	Any
Aim	To cater for auditory learning styles; to practise sound-symbol relationships
Duration	2 minutes (depending on length of text)
Materials	A reading text from the coursebook
Skills / Language	Pronunciation

Procedure
The next time you come to a reading text, once you have finished with the comprehension exercises, explain that you would like the students to read the text aloud. This would be the most standard procedure:

- Before the students read aloud, ask them to underline the words in a sentence they think will sound louder (i.e. receive main stress). These words are usually the last noun, verb, adjective or adverb.
- Nominate a student to begin reading.
- After a sentence or two, nominate a different student to continue.
- Continue randomly across the room, so that everyone is following the text at the same time.

Variations
A Chorus Line
Follow the standard procedure above, but every so often have the whole class read a line from the text. Then go back to individual students.

In Pairs: 1
Have the students face each other and begin reading the text, taking turns. This way everyone is reading at the same time.

In Pairs: 2
Have the students face each other and read the text together. If one or the other notices a pronunciation mistake, they should stop and start the same sentence again.

Mark It Up
Tell the students to select a paragraph and mark with a line where they would pause while reading (e.g. after full stops, commas, etc.). Then nominate different students to read.

Quickly, Slowly, with Feeling
With a dialogue, or with individual sentences, ask the students to vary the way they read the text. Ask them to read it faster, more slowly, with passion, in a whisper, as a shout, with anger.

Listen and Recap

Level	Any
Aim	To cater for auditory learning styles; to check understanding
Duration	2 minutes
Materials	None
Skills / Language	Speaking; rephrasing and summarising

Procedure

1 The next time you are giving an explanation of a grammar / vocabulary point, pause after the first part of your explanation and ask the students to turn to a partner.

2 Give them the following instructions:
- Tell them to tell their partner everything they have understood about whatever you were explaining.
- Tell them to stop after a couple of minutes.

3 Go on with your explanation.

4 Repeat the procedure at the end of the explanation.

Variation

This activity doesn't need to be restricted to students recapping what you have been saying – they could equally well do this after reading an explanation of a grammar point. Many coursebooks have pages devoted to language reference (with full explanations of the grammar points). The students can read and recap in the same manner.

NOTE: Lower-level students can be allowed to recap in their own language.

Musical Writing

Level	From elementary onwards
Aim	To cater for auditory learning styles; to stimulate students to write with a musical prompt
Duration	20 minutes
Materials	Extracts of instrumental music (no lyrics) lasting one or two minutes
Skills / Language	Writing; tenses and other language useful for narration

Preparation

Make a recording of an appropriate piece of music. It can be fast or slow, classical or modern, happy or sad, etc.

Procedure

1 Tell the class you are going to play them a piece of music and that they have to think of a story that goes with it.

2 Write the following questions on the board:
Where does the story take place?
Who are the people in the story?
Are they young or old?
What are they doing?
How do they feel?

3 Ask the students to listen to the music and take notes.

4 When the music is over, give them time to fill out their stories and make any changes they wish. At the end of this phase they should have notes that tell a story, however incomplete.

5 The students turn to a partner (or partners) and, referring to their notes, they tell their stories, using present or past tenses:
John is walking along the street when he meets Julia.
John was walking along the street when he met Julia.

Follow-up

The students can use their notes to write up their story for homework (or to co-construct a group story in class).

NOTES: Encourage the students to take **notes** as they listen, rather than full sentences (unless they actually **prefer** to write full sentences). Some students may prefer to take notes in their mother tongue, which is fine too, as the end product will be in English.

Encourage those students who haven't managed to write very much to borrow ideas from those who have written more when the students exchange stories using their notes.

Musical Variations

Level	From elementary onwards
Aim	To cater for auditory learning styles; to stimulate students to write with a musical prompt
Duration	Variable
Materials	Extracts of instrumental music (no lyrics) lasting one or two minutes
Skills / Language	Writing; tenses and other language useful for narration

Variation 1

1 The students listen to three or four very different extracts of music.

2 You pause for a minute or so after each extract (remember to refer to them by their number: 1, 2, 3, etc.).

3 They write what comes to mind. If necessary, prompt them with *who, what, where, when, why*.

4 When all extracts have been played, the students read out their notes at random and the class has to guess which extract the student is describing.

5 They choose at least one set of notes to write as a complete composition for homework.

6 In class, give the students a chance to read each other's work and try to identify which piece of music 'inspired' the composition.

Variation 2

1 For homework, the students write a narrative composition inspired by a piece of music of their own choice. It could be a fast exciting piece of music (e.g. Rossini's *William Tell* overture) or a slow romantic piece (e.g. Beethoven's *Moonlight Sonata*).

2 The students bring their homework to class, with a recording of the musical extract which inspired the composition.

3 You choose a composition and either ask the student-writer to read it out or you read it out, correcting discreetly as you read.

4 The students listen and answer the following questions: *Can you guess what kind of music inspired this story? Was it fast or slow? Was it happy or sad?*

Variation 3

1 Prepare stem sentences for the beginning of each paragraph of a story. For example:
Paragraph 1
Julia will never forget the day she met Robert ...
Paragraph 2
Later that evening ...
Paragraph 3
At last they decided ...
Paragraph 4
Years later ...

For each paragraph, choose a piece of music lasting about a minute.

2 In the lesson, write the first stem on the board and play the matching piece of music. The students listen and take notes on what they imagine is happening in the story. For example:
Julia will never forget the day she met Robert; it was a warm sunny day and she was out walking in the park ...

3 Pause after each extract to give the students time to jot down notes inspired by the music.

4 Write the next stem sentence on the board (or dictate it).

5 Play the next extract and ask the students to write down what the extract brings to mind, as before.

6 Continue this procedure for all the extracts.

7 When the listening and note-taking phase is complete, ask the students to turn to their partners and tell their story, using the notes they have made as a guide.

8 For homework, they write up their story in full, incorporating any useful ideas or language they have picked up from their partner.

Musical Timekeeping

Level	Any
Aim	To cater for auditory learning styles; to mark the beginning / end of an activity
Duration	3–4 minutes
Materials	A series of three- / four-minute songs (pop songs are good for this)
Language / Skills	Varied

Procedure

1 The next time you set a quiet activity (like a grammar exercise or a short writing exercise) that requires a time limit, tell the students they should complete the activity before a song finishes.

2 Put the song on quietly and let the students get on with their work.

3 When the song is finished, stop the cassette or CD and tell them to put down their pens.

NOTE: If the students know the song, they will automatically hear when it is coming to an end and will be finishing off.

Mime Scenes

Level	Any
Aim	To cater for kinaesthetic learning styles; to revise language from the coursebook
Duration	20 minutes
Materials	Slips of paper with sentences from the coursebook
Language / Skills	Present simple / past simple

Preparation

Write sentences from the coursebook on slips of paper.

Procedure

1 Take a narrative text from the coursebook before students have done it in class. Write the main elements of the story on separate slips of paper, like this:

Jane and Roger met at a party.
They went out together.
They fell in love.
They wrote love letters.
They got married.
They have two children.
They are very happy.

2 Give the slips out in random order to pairs of students.

3 The pairs prepare to mime what is on their slip of paper (e.g. meeting someone, falling in love, going out together, and so on).

4 The class watches each mime in turn and takes notes.

5 When all the extracts have been mimed, the pairs recall and write down what happened and put the events in a logical order.

6 Elicit from the pairs what they think is the correct order.

7 The whole class recreates the story as a whole-class activity.

8 The students check their answers with the reading text in the coursebook.

Variation

The students can mime the story for each other in groups.

Matching Mimes

Level	From intermediate onwards
Aim	To cater for kinaesthetic learning styles; to practise vocabulary (jobs) and adjectives for describing people
Duration	Variable
Materials	Two sets of cards (adjectives and nouns)
Language / Skills	Vocabulary practice: adjectives + proper nouns (jobs)

Preparation

Choose a set of adjectives for describing people from the coursebook. Add some of your own to complete the set. For example:

sleepy   loving   angry   proud   shy   energetic

Write out the adjectives and the nouns referring to jobs on two sets of cards: A and B.

Procedure

1 Pre-teach the adjectives.

2 Place the cards in two piles face down on the table at the front of the class. For example:

A Cards
loving   angry   proud   shy   energetic
hungry   thirsty   drunken   sleepy   clumsy

B Cards
postman   teacher   doctor   nurse   ballet dancer
carpenter   tailor   policeman   electrician   athlete
vicar

3 The first student comes to the front and takes a card from each pile and mimes the combination. The class has to guess the situation. For example:

You're a drunken ballet dancer / an energetic carpenter.

Variation

Give the students a handout with a list of combinations based on the adjectives and nouns above. Ask them to do the 'mine and guess' activity in pairs. For example:

- a sleepy vicar
- a proud teacher
- an angry postman
- a hungry doctor.

Knees, Waist, Shoulders

Level	From elementary onwards
Aim	To cater for kinaesthetic learning styles; to revise the three parts of irregular verbs
Duration	Variable
Materials	None
Language / Skills	Irregular verbs

Procedure

1 Ask the class to stand up.

2 One student stands in front of the class and says the three parts of an irregular verb. For example:
bring   brought   brought

They accompany each part with a gesture (touch knees, hands on waist, hands on shoulders).

3 The class copies the actions, repeating the three parts of the verb as they do so.

Variation

Prepare the following sets of slips:

Set 1
Write the **first** part of irregular verbs.

Set 2
Write the **first two** parts of the verb.

Set 3
Write **all three** parts of the verb.

As the students come to the front to perform their mime, they choose a number (1, 2 or 3), according to how easy or difficult they want the task to be. You give them an appropriate slip.

Vocabulary Relay

Level	Any
Aim	To cater for kinaesthetic learning styles; to revise lexical sets
Duration	10 minutes
Materials	Word cards
Language / Skills	Lexical sets (*furniture, food, travel, sports, hobbies*, etc.)

Preparation
Prepare three sets of cards:
Set 1: furniture words
Set 2: animal words
Set 3: sports and hobbies

Procedure

1 Draw a table with three headings on the board, like this:

Furniture	Animals	Sports and Hobbies

2 Divide the class into two teams. Each team has a different coloured chalk or board pen.

3 Put the three sets of cards on the table.

4 A student from each team comes to the front, takes a card, goes to the board and writes the word on the card in the correct category.

5 When the first student has sat down (or passed the chalk / board pen to the next member of the team) the next student gets up, goes to the front, picks up a card and writes the word on the board in the correct category.

6 The process is repeated, till the teacher calls *Time's up!* The table should now look like this:

Furniture	Animals	Sports and Hobbies
chair table stool	*dog cat mouse rabbit cow sheep*	*swimming chess music stamp-collecting basketball painting*

7 Declare the winning team the one which has written most words on the board.

8 Make sure everyone knows the words on the board and ask if they can add more.

Rub Them Out

Level	From intermediate onwards
Aim	To cater for kinaesthetic learning styles; to check understanding of vocabulary
Duration	Variable
Materials	None
Language / Skills	Vocabulary encountered or to be encountered

Preparation
Make a list of words the students should know, bearing in mind the diverse levels in the class.

Procedure

1 Put a list of easy / difficult words on the board in random order (keep a paper copy of the words for yourself).

2 Divide the class into two teams.

3 The students (one from each team) take it in turns to come to the board and explain one word they think they know. If they do it successfully, they rub it out.

4 As the game progresses, the words left on the board will become more difficult.

5 The winner is the team which explains and rubs out the last word.

NOTE: This activity allows the less able students to take part (they can choose the easier words to explain) but also allows the cleverer ones in each team to end up doing the final words. The kinaesthetic element will appeal to those students who get bored with sitting down at their desks doing vocabulary exercises.

One Teacher, One Class

Nominating

One of the problems with mixed-ability level is that stronger students tend to call out the answers all the time. To avoid this, you can nominate students.

- Ask the question first, followed by the student's name. This way all the students have to listen out for their name.
- Ask more challenging questions to the stronger students and less challenging questions to the weaker ones.
- Vary the way you nominate students to answer questions. Don't simply start at one end of the class and move in order to the other end. Students may 'switch off' if they know it isn't their turn for a while.
- Keep a record of who you have been asking recently. It is easy to fall into a rhythm of nominating the same students again and again.
- A particularly effective use of nomination is to address students by their name when you have your back turned to the class – for example, when you are writing on the board or adjusting the CD. It sends a message to the class that you are aware of the members of the group and are in control of the group dynamics. This strategy confirms the old adage about good teachers 'having eyes in the back of their head'.
- Remember: nominating can be done by other means apart from actually using a student's name. You can use eye contact and even (occasionally) pointing – in a non-threatening way – to let students know you'd like them to speak.
- Remember, too, that most people like hearing their first name being mentioned. Apart from its usefulness in distributing contributions fairly, nominating is also good for rapport and 'lowering the affective filter' – i.e. helping students feel more welcome and relaxed.

Naming students may seem to be a minor detail in the context of the sea of difficulties teachers face, but it is important to bear in mind that the big picture is made up of details, a little bit like an impressionist painting.

Correcting

Correction is more of an issue with teachers than nominating, but it is nevertheless a much-misunderstood and abused process. Correction implies that there is something 'wrong' which has to be put right; and this in a sense is true. On the other hand, it is important to exorcise the stigma from 'making errors' and to see error correction as a necessary and positive aspect of learning a language. We have always found it more constructive to refer to steps in learning or 'good tries' rather than errors and to make of correction a flexible instrument for encouraging learners and building their confidence rather than making them feel small and inadequate. Let us look more closely at how this can be done.

When doing correction in an open-class format, it is important to 'spread it around'.

- Avoid the 'One Right Answer' syndrome whereby the teacher seeks to get the Right Answer as quickly as possible, usually from the best students. Allow students thinking time and prompt them, if necessary, to help them come up with either the right answer or a reasonable alternative to the right answer!
- Distinguish between instant correction (where communication has broken down) and delayed correction (which you deliver later to the whole class after monitoring pair and group activities).
- Use rephrasing to correct errors, so you don't interrupt the flow of conversation. This is unobtrusive and gives the student natural feedback without reducing their self-esteem. The technique involves slipping into your discourse a piece of language the student got wrong, but in its correct form.
- There will obviously be more to correct from the weaker students, so don't forget to correct stronger students as well.
- Pronunciation is an obvious candidate for correction of stronger students. By correcting them on aspects such as sounds, word stress and intonation, you are pushing stronger students to perform even better.
- Build correction feedback into follow-up activities so students see their 'good tries' recontextualised and made constructive use of; it is one thing to identify someone's errors and another to make use of those errors in building new activities and model texts.
- Remember to use the full range of teacher correction techniques but also self-correction and peer correction techniques, when appropriate.

Correction has a central role to play in language teaching; it has rich possibilities. It is well known that correction is good for building students' accuracy but it is less widely acknowledged that correction can also be good for building students' self-esteem. Finally, it is often forgotten that there are times when we should give correction a rest, especially when students are in full flow or struggling to achieve some kind of flow.

Grouping

If you are giving different tasks to different-level students, you must make sure you group the students accordingly.

- For collaborative work: pair weak and strong students together and ask the strong one to help the weaker one.
- For team activities (such as quizzes or games): ensure that there is a balance of students in each group.
- For extendable tasks, or tasks that have options for early finishers: group the students according to ability.
- For group tasks: add a **specific** instruction, if necessary, so that everyone must participate (e.g. by writing two sentences **each**).
- Build an interactive element into mixed groups so strong and quiet students are obliged to work together to complete the task. Make them dependent on each other for the completion of the task.
- Make getting into groups a fun activity, to help overcome students' reluctance to change position.

Variety in the groupings in your lessons is crucial – be wary of letting two people always work together.

Monitoring

It is vital to circulate and monitor mixed-ability groups carefully, in a discreet and unthreatening manner.

- If you see that a student is being left out because they can't keep up, intervene and try to bring them back into the group.
- If you see a student is getting bored, intervene and encourage them to help the others.
- Don't interfere if students seem not to want to be monitored; give them the option of letting you know if they want to be 'helped' or monitored.
- Get students to do the monitoring by building in an information-exchange element to your activities.
- Get students to report their partner's answers rather than just giving their own answers – this spreads out the monitoring between you and the students.
- Build in a writing element to the group tasks where appropriate – this facilitates the monitoring process by giving you access to the outcome of the task in hand.
- Discreetly move **away** from the student who is speaking or about to speak so that your field of control is defined and extended:
  by your voice (directing comments or questions to different areas of the class)
  by your position (alerting students who might otherwise feel at a safe distance)
  by eye contact (most of the class should be within view for most of the time).

Monitoring is a particular challenge in large classes and it is therefore important to combine it with the whole range of group formations: whole-class work, pair work and group work; it also means you need to use the space in the classroom creatively, by moving around and getting a different perspective on the class. Remember: varying your position around the room not only refreshes the class by building in an element of surprise but it extends your control over the dynamics of the group. It also gives you an insight into what is going on in forgotten corners of the room.

Giving Time to Think

One cannot stress too greatly the importance of giving students thinking time – especially the 'quiet' ones. 'Quiet' students can be observed to find their voice given a bit of time and appropriate prompting.

- Give weaker students time to answer. So that the lesson doesn't drag, fill the 'thinking time' with prompts and clues to help the student come up with the right answer.
- Use the thinking time to remind students of previous knowledge on which they can build to acquire the new knowledge.
- Re-channel questions to the rest of the class to keep them involved and then return to the original student, who will in the meantime have gathered hints to help them come up with the right answer.

Rushing students and setting time limits is a hall mark of a 'testing' mode of teaching; it often leads to stress and failure. Good teaching recognises the importance of giving students an appropriate amount of time in which to dig up their often submerged or emergent knowledge.

Asking and Listening to Each Other

Students are used to thinking that the teacher is the only person worth listening to in class; this is part of the traditional view of the teacher as the fount of all wisdom. Though there is a time and place for the teacher to give information and explanations (both vital roles), we should also try to teach students to learn from each other. To do this, they must be allowed to ask questions as well as to answer them. They should also be encouraged to accept that they can learn from peers as well as from teachers.

- Avoid the 'interrogation'-type lesson: give the students plenty of opportunities to **ask** as well as to **answer** questions. This may require a few minutes before the activity for students to prepare their own questions on a particular topic (e.g. *The five questions I would like a TV interviewer to ask me ...*).

- Make checking and cross-checking a regular feature of the class. This way you focus attention and encourage involvement (particularly on the part of more advanced students who tend to get bored easily).
- Ask questions like *Do you agree?* or instruct students to repeat what somebody has just said or carry on from where the previous speaker stopped.
- Get them to report back on what their partner has said, not only their own answers.
- Encourage activities which in their outcome incorporate the views or answers of other students – this makes asking questions and listening to responses a natural part of the task in hand.

Students will often 'switch off' unless a question is specifically asked of them. Setting up activities where they both ask and answer questions will help reduce discipline problems; question and answer routines both fill a dangerous vacuum and also activate students' self-esteem – they feel more in control of the foreign language.

Reviewing and Recycling
It is particularly important in classes of different levels, where some students may be moving ahead at a different pace from other students, to give weaker students plenty of opportunities to revisit the same language.

- Use learner-produced quizzes, where the questions are at least in part provided by the better students.
- Use texts produced by the better students as the basis for creating revision material in the form of gap-fills, re-ordering or transformation tasks.
- Pause during the lesson and get students to recap on what has been done in class so far.

The challenge is to give one group of students further exposure to the same language without losing the interest of the students who are in less need of reviewing the material.

As Many As You Can

Level	Any
Aim	To encourage flexible input; to personalise structure practice
Duration	5 minutes
Materials	None
Skills / Language	Writing; adjective + preposition structures

Procedure

1 Take a suitable sentence item from your coursebook. It should be something that is easily personalised. It is best to start with *I ...* , *My family ...* , or *People in my country ...* . For example:
> *I'm afraid of _____.*

2 Elicit examples of words or phrases that could go in the slot.
> *I'm afraid of spiders.*
> *I'm afraid of flying.*
> *I'm afraid of walking in the town centre at night.*

3 Write on the board:
> *I'm afraid of _____.*
> *I'm not afraid of _____.*

4 Tell the students to complete these sentences in as many ways as they can in three minutes. Encourage the students who usually finish early to also try and write *longer* phrases in the slot.

5 At the end of three minutes, tell them to stop writing and to compare their answers with a partner. Don't ask how many sentences they wrote, as this is **not** the objective of the exercise.

6 Elicit different examples from the class.

Variations
You can use this activity with any number of structures. For example:

Past Simple	*Yesterday I ... and I didn't ...*
Present Perfect	*I have ... and I haven't ever ...*
Relative Clauses	*I like / I don't like things that ...*
Future	*I'm definitely / I am never going to ...*

NOTE: By giving a topic that students can relate to and by being flexible with the output required, you avoid the problem of early finishers as students of differing levels can finish at the same time and still carry out an interactive exchange as 'equals' in a final stage.

Team Testing

Level	Any
Aim	To test each other on grammar
Duration	15 minutes
Materials	A coursebook grammar table
Language / Skills	Varied

Procedure

1 Copy a grammar table from the book you are using onto the board. For example, here is a typical coursebook presentation of polar questions in the present simple:

Question	Positive	Negative
Do you like ice-cream?	Yes, I do.	No, I don't.
Does she like football?	Yes, she does.	No, she doesn't.
Do they like television?	Yes, they do.	No, they don't.

2 Divide the class into two teams.

3 Ask two 'weak' students to come to the front, representing the two teams.

4 Ask the rest of each team to close their eyes or turn away from the board.

5 Each student at the board chooses a word or two to erase from any of the columns.

6 The teams open their eyes or turn round. Each team gets time to consult and then must call out the missing words. The students at the board write the words back in, but only if they are correct.

The teams get a point for every word correctly written back up on the board.

Variations

Alternatively, **you** can erase the material from the board, in which case the 'weak' students should be asked to recall the first items erased, rather than the later ones.

You can apply the same technique to a board full of vocabulary-to-be-revised. Again, a 'weak' learner can be the 'eraser'.

NOTE: If students are uncooperative about closing their eyes or turning away from the board you, or the 'erasers', can gradually erase more and more of the material on the board and thus make the task more of a memory game.

Oral Concertina

Level	From elementary onwards
Aim	To retell a text cooperatively
Duration	15 minutes
Materials	A story
Language / Skills	Narrative tenses; listening and speaking

Procedure

1 Tell the students a story from the coursebook you are using or ask them to read one.

2 Begin to retell the story or ask one of the 'better' students to do this. One sentence is enough.

3 Choose another student at random to continue the story from the point at which the previous student left off.

4 The second student may add as little or as much as he / she is comfortable with. A word is enough. A sentence is fine.

5 Nominate a third student to continue the story from where the second student left off.

The process of building up the story continues in this manner.

Follow-up

When the story has been reconstructed orally in the manner described above, the students can write a summary, either in groups or for homework.

Variation

The class can be divided into two teams who compete to reconstruct the story. The teams alternate in adding the next part of the story.

NOTE: Using nomination ensures both the flow of the story and the participation of students of diverse levels. Accepting all contributions, long and short, is crucial to the process of encouraging all students' self-esteem.

Scattered Texts

Level	From elementary onwards
Aim	To retell a text in a collaborative jigsaw task
Duration	20 minutes
Materials	A text from the coursebook; slips of paper
Language / Skills	Listening

Preparation

Copy a text onto slips of paper, one slip for each student in the class. The sentence on each slip should follow on to form a coherent text, like this:

> Once there was a farmer who lived in the Amazon forest.

> He liked climbing tall trees.

> One day, he was climbing a tree when he found a large nest.

> In the nest, there were three large eggs which belonged to an eagle.

> He took one of the eggs.

Procedure

1 Give out the sentences to the students in random order, but choosing the easier ones for the 'slower' learners and the more difficult ones for the 'faster' ones.

2 Ask the students to read their sentence and decide if it is the first sentence of the text. The 'owner' of the first sentence reads it out loud.

3 The students listen and decide whether their sentence comes next. They read it aloud.

4 Continue until you have constructed as much of the text as you want.

5 The students hand in their slips and, in groups, they reconstruct the text in writing.

Variations

This task can be done in two ways:
- **after** students have read the text in the coursebook as revision or reconstruction.
- **before** they read the text in the book as 'prevision' or 'preconstruction'.

Disappearing Texts

Level	From elementary onwards
Aim	To reduce and then recreate a text in collaboration
Duration	10 minutes
Materials	A coursebook text or one you have prepared
Language / Skills	Varied

Procedure

1 Write a text, either one of your own or one taken from the coursebook, on the board. For example:

> *Akis and Stefanos, the terrible twins who were born in Greece on 22 August 1983, were playing football outside in the street with their best friend, Vayios, who was twelve, when suddenly Akis kicked the ball too hard and, with a loud smash, broke their neighbour's window.*

2 Ask one of the 'weaker' students to come to the board and rub out between one and three words from the text.

3 Tell the student to read out loud the text they have reduced. Ask if it is still 'grammatically correct' – if it isn't, ask others to suggest what words should go back in. Ensure that the remaining text is still grammatically correct before continuing.

4 Continue with other students taking turns to come up, erase words and read out the text. The more text is erased from the board, the more difficult the task becomes. This is when you start calling on the 'stronger' students to erase words.

5 When the text has shrunk as much as it possibly can, put the students in pairs.

6 Ask them to reconstruct it from memory and write it down.

Variation

Alternatively, you can do a 'disappearing dialogue' which can be personalised in terms of the students' own experience.

Acknowledgement: This Variation is based on an idea by Jim Rose, English Teaching *professional* Issue 5.

DIY Questionnaire

Level	From elementary onwards
Aim	To use learner input to personalise questionnaires for grammar revision
Duration	15 minutes
Materials	Pencil and paper
Language / Skills	Varied

Procedure

1 Do a 'Find Someone Who' activity in the normal way.

2 Give the students a blank questionnaire on a topic relevant to the class.

3 Tell the students to complete as many of the blanks as they can with the names of hobbies and sports that they would like to know more about. For example:

Hobbies and Sports	
I'd like to find someone who:	**Name**
1 (likes skateboarding)	(John)
2 (has been rock climbing)	(Maria)
3 (goes scuba diving)	(Peter)

4 Ask them to add more examples of hobbies by sharing ideas with other students until they have completed as many of the ten spaces in the table as they can.

5 They then ask other students their questions and write in the name of any students who give an affirmative answer. For example:

> **Student A:** *Do you like skateboarding?*
> **Student B:** *No, I don't.*
> **Student A:** *Do you like skateboarding?*
> **Student C:** *Yes, I do.*

Student A writes the name of Student C in the 'Name' column in the questionnaire.

6 When time is up (say five minutes of question and answer), get feedback by asking the students with most names in the name column to give the class some feedback on their results. For example:

> **Student A:** *John likes skateboarding. Maria has been rock climbing.*

7 Round off the task by asking the students to write a brief report of what they have found out about their fellow students as a result of conducting the questionnaire.

Party Gossip

Level	Any
Aim	To introduce flexibility into speaking practice
Duration	20 minutes
Materials	Split two-part exchanges on slips of paper; blank slips of paper; party music (optional)
Language / Skills	Varied

Preparation

Write out slips consisting of a question and an answer that could lead on to a conversation. The questions / answers should form pairs. For example:

Where did you leave your wallet?	In my handbag.
How much do you earn?	I'd rather not tell you.

Procedure

1 Write example *wh-* questions and answers on the board:
> *Where did you get that hat?*   *I bought it at Zara.*
> *Where's Helen?*   *I don't know. I haven't seen her for ages.*

2 Hand out blank slips of paper and ask the students to write their own questions and answers on separate slips.

3 Collect in the students' questions and answers and mix them up with the examples you have prepared.

4 Give each student a slip of paper containing either a question or an answer.

Who's that guy over there?	That's Brad Pitt.

5 Ask the students to memorise their sentence.

6 Ask them to get up and mingle as if they were at a party (you can have party-like music playing softly in the background).

7 They say their line to whoever they meet at 'the party' and, when they find their other half, they stop and chat. The aim is to have a chatty, gossipy conversation 'just to pass the time'.

8 If they finish early, they go round in pairs and mingle with other pairs, 'gossiping' about the other members of the group. Alternatively, you can ask them to sit down while the other members of the group are still chatting and to write down their question and answer followed by the dialogue they had.

Ranking

Level	From elementary onwards
Aim	To exploit students' preferences and opinions
Duration	20 minutes
Materials	A list of topic-related lexical items or statements
Language / Skills	Speaking; note taking

Preparation
Prepare a list of topic-related lexical items or statements.

Procedure
1 Explain to the class that they are going to discuss a problem by listing a number of items in order of preference. For example:

How to survive on a desert island

2 Elicit a random list of items which the students think they might need and draw up a list on the board. For example:

sleeping bag   aspirins   knife   camera
sunglasses   raincoat   clock

3 Add some of items of your own to the list to ensure that there is a balance of easy and difficult vocabulary.

4 Ask the students to choose a minimum of three items and put them in order of usefulness in the particular situation. 'Better' students may choose more items if they wish.

5 Ask them to jot down notes next to the items they have chosen, glossing the reasons why they think the items would be useful.

6 Ask them to turn to a partner and exchange views. They should take notes as they listen.

Variations
Ranking activities are very flexible. Other topics suitable for such activities could be:

- the best forms of transport
- an appropriate sentence for minor or more serious crimes
- the most important qualities of a good teacher / learner / friend.

NOTES: All students have opinions and they are all equally valuable, whether the English of any particular student is 'strong' or 'weak'. The eliciting stage is another example of learner input, a useful device in mixed-level classes. The final stage gives the weak students the opportunity to extend their lists by drawing naturally on the work of others.

They're the Experts

Level	From elementary onwards
Aim	To draw on students' general knowledge
Duration	30 minutes
Materials	Student-based questions
Language / Skills	Interrogative forms

Procedure
1 Ask the students to write two or three quiz questions, based on general knowledge topics (they can do this in class or for homework, alone or in pairs or groups). For example: *history, geography, pop music, sport, films,* etc.

2 Collect in the questions.

3 Divide the class into teams.

4 Conduct the quiz, using the students' questions (as you read out the questions, you should silently correct any linguistic errors, but without further comment).

Variation
Take home the questions prepared in class and type them up correctly as a sheet of, say, twenty questions. Give each student (or team) a copy of the questions. This will not only allow students to conduct the quiz themselves (acting as quizmasters, asking the other team questions), but will also provide useful feedback on student errors.

NOTE: Students are usually very happy to show you how much they know about things that are important to them or that they are good at, and if they are allowed to share their knowledge in your English class, their interest and participation (and self-esteem!) are guaranteed.

4

Homework

'The number one problem with homework is that they just don't do it.'

For students, homework should ideally consolidate work done in class. Additionally, it should provide an opportunity for them to review problem areas, as well as working at their own pace and in their own way. This is one goal of homework. Another goal is to extend learning outside class. This means developing study skills which will help students take more independent responsibility for their learning.

Homework should also allow you, as teacher, to do the following things:

- carry out activities that are more motivating because you can link them with the real world and the students' own interests
- save valuable class time for other activities which can only be done in class
- show students you value their work through the way you give feedback on the homework.

Time and again, however, the same complaints about homework arise. The number one complaint is, of course, that students simply **don't do it**. This is followed closely by copying. Here are some reasons we believe that this happens:

- Homework is seen as a punishment, or useless and irrelevant.

- Homework is seen as mechanical (in fact the more mechanical it is, the easier it is to copy).
- The homework is boring, too difficult or too easy.
- The homework is covered in corrections or just given a mark, both of which may lower students' self-esteem.
- Students don't have enough time to do the homework.

Thus, homework ends up as a kind of hide-and-seek between teacher and learner. How can we begin to overcome this attitude and make the most of a unique opportunity for extending and enriching the learning of English?

4.1 Valuing Homework

'I suspect my students don't do the homework because they think it's boring and useless.'

The activities in the first section of this chapter are about setting the groundwork for good homework. A good starting point is to show your students that you place a high value on the homework they do. If you leave assigning homework for the last minute in class, if you collect homework and don't return it (or return it late), if you assign homework irregularly, then it is much more likely that students will reciprocate in like manner.

You should, therefore, find out from the students what works best for **them**. How much time do they have for homework? What are they interested in, both in class and out of class? What do they need? How do they learn things best on their own?

4.2 Linking Homework to Classwork

'I only give the workbook for homework – and they never do it.'

The activities in the second section of this chapter give suggestions on motivating kinds of homework that link to classwork. There are ways of making homework a collaborative, cooperative activity rather than a lonely grind.

Homework will be seen as more important if the link with classwork is visible. This can be done:

- from class to home – by starting something in class and finishing it at home
- from home to class – by doing something at home and bringing it to class.

This doesn't mean avoiding the workbook (if your students are using one), but making the link stronger. If homework is seen as integral to what happens in class, it may be easier to build an intrinsic motive for doing it: if students don't do it, they experience at first hand, in class, the impact of this non-compliance. This is a much more effective 'carrot' than simply preaching about the virtues of homework or expressing threats and / or disappointment when students fail to do their out-of-class work.

4.3 Correcting Homework

'I don't think they ever actually read my comments. They don't learn anything from my corrections – I correct because I feel I have to.'

This section focuses on the integral part correction techniques play in making homework a purposeful learning activity. Indeed, students often see teachers as full-time correction machines. We think it's important to put the human factor back into the machine – and to put the student in the centre of the cycle:

classwork → correction
homework → follow-up

Many teachers opt for a zero tolerance policy towards deviant language and make life not only more difficult for themselves but also miss many opportunities for making the learners more active players in the process of learning.

So as you try to get them to participate more in their learning process, why not find out from the students themselves how they like their homework to be corrected? Even if you decide not to act on everything they would like you to do, the very process of going to the students and asking them to express their preferences is very good for rapport, positive attitudes and participation (or RAP, for short).

4.4 Following Up Homework

'I don't have time to mark thirty pieces of homework!'

The activities in this last section illustrate ways of 'recycling' the students' work to give it new life and value.

Homework needn't always be marked and controlled by **you**. Students can be encouraged and trained to self-correct and edit their own homework and that of their peers. You can also use models of homework to foster learning. This doesn't necessarily mean using only the best homework, either. If you use the 'worst' student's homework as a vehicle for learning for the whole class, this is the most effective way of 'valuing' that student's work. Many teachers, metaphorically at least, toss students' work into the dustbin by covering it in negative marks and remarks.

It is what we do outside class on a regular, habit-forming basis that makes the difference in language learning; reading an English-language newspaper or magazine as a matter of routine, listening to songs and other audio material in the target language, watching DVDs, keeping a notebook of useful expressions, interacting with other English users either face-to-face, by e-mail or in chatrooms, and so on.

The challenge is how to activate this huge out-of-class resource. The activities and techniques here illustrate a general but vital strategy: to make the homework appear to be useful.

Homework Survey

Level	Any
Aim	To get students to think about homework
Duration	10 minutes (in class)
Materials	Homework Survey (see page 91 opposite)
Skills / Language	Reading; speaking

Preparation

Make enough copies of the Homework Survey for each student.

Procedure

1 At the end of the lesson, distribute the surveys so that each student has one. Ask them to complete the survey for homework. Tell them not to complete the final *To be completed in class* section yet.

2 In the next lesson, ask the students to work in pairs and compare their answers.

3 Ask the pairs to come up with three types of homework task that they feel have worked for them in the past. Tell them to write these down at the bottom of the survey in the *To be completed in class* box.

4 Collect in the surveys.

Follow-up

You now have a selection of ideas for homework that students have at least expressed approval of and, implicitly, a willingness to do. You can decide what to do with the survey. Here are some suggestions:

- Go through the results of the survey with the class and highlight the top three types of homework students expressed a willingness to do. Assign one of those types of homework first.
- Write and post up a list of the types of homework you are going to assign throughout the year.
- Write and post up a list of homework tasks and each class puts a tick next to the ones the students have done. Review this list with the students from time to time to show them what they have achieved.
- Half way through the year, come back to the original survey and ask the students if they would like to change anything and if they feel they have been doing useful homework.

Variation

For very low levels, the students could be encouraged to do the activity in their own language.

Homework Survey

Tick (✔) the option which is true for you:

I usually do my homework:

    at home ☐

    in the library ☐

    at work ☐

    other _____

I usually do my homework:

    alone ☐

    with a friend ☐

    with someone from my family ☐

    other _____

I usually do my homework:

    in the morning ☐

    in the afternoon ☐

    at night ☐

    other _____

I usually do my homework:

    in bits and pieces ☐

    all in one go ☐

    a long time before the deadline ☐

    just before the deadline ☐

I listen to music when I do my homework.

    true ☐   false ☐

I like doing homework.

    true ☐   false ☐

Tick (✔) the kind of homework you would like to do more of.

    grammar exercises ☐

    learning new words ☐

    exercises in the workbook ☐

    internet-related activities ☐

    practising exam questions ☐

Tick (✔) the kind of things you would like to write.

    letters / e-mails ☐

    stories ☐

    reports ☐

    essays ☐

    other _____

Tick (✔) the kind of things you would like to read.

    stories ☐

    poems ☐

    news stories ☐

    academic texts ☐

    other _____

To be completed in class. Please leave blank.

Three kinds of useful homework we have done:

_____

_____

_____

Dealing with Difficulties © Lindsay Clandfield and Luke Prodromou published by DELTA PUBLISHING

Homework Log

Level	Any
Aim	To keep a record of homework
Duration	10 minutes (first class), 3 minutes (each you assign homework)
Materials	An exercise book for each student
Skills / Language	Writing

Procedure

1 Ask each student to buy an exercise book for their homework.

2 At the beginning of the course, set aside ten minutes and ask the students to make a title page for their 'homework log'. On the title page they should write their name, the class, the class times, their phone number and / or e-mail address.

3 Tell the students to find another student in the class who will be their 'homework contact'. If a student misses a class, they can find out about any homework assigned from their homework contact. They should write their homework contact's name and number in their log.

4 On the second page of the log, ask them to make three columns, one for the homework assigned, one for the date due and one marked 'Done'. See example below.

5 Each time you assign homework, ask the students to record it in their logs. Tell them to tick the homework when they have finished it.

Variations

You can add other columns, such as 'Mark received'.

For Young Learners

You can make copies of the title page for a homework log. The students can further decorate the title page by colouring it, or pasting other pictures on it.

You can also use this book to communicate with their parents. At the bottom of each page you can add comments about the student's behaviour (good or bad) and work done in class. You can ask parents to sign the book as well (especially for younger learners).

NOTE: Keeping the homework in one exercise book means that you can collect all the books from time to time to check them.

Homework Assigned	Date Due	Done
Write a letter introducing yourself to the teacher.	March 24	✔
Write a description of a family member.	April 1	✔
Complete unit 4 of the workbook.	April 8	

Check After, Check Before

Level	Any
Aim	To raise awareness of the value of homework; to help students learn from their mistakes
Duration	5–10 minutes (in class)
Materials	A handout on writing problems to give students at the beginning of the year
Skills / Language	Writing; self-editing

Preparation

Create a checklist for students to use to self-check their homework. The ones in the examples opposite are for an elementary and an intermediate class, but you can make one for the level of your students and the typical mistakes they make.

Procedure

1 Give the students the checklist and go through the meaning of each item. Tell them that you will always be looking out for these things in their homework, too.

2 Mark the students' homework in the usual way, but make sure you indicate their errors in a clear manner: underlining, writing what the problem is, using codes, etc. See Proofreading on page 71 for the use of codes in correction.

3 As you give them their homework back, ask the students to take out their original checklist.

4 Tell them to go through their homework and tick off any relevant points from the checklist.

5 Ask them to use the checklist when they do their next piece of homework. They should check their homework **before** they give it in each time, from now on.

NOTE: This task helps students focus on and learn from their errors. It raises awareness not only about the language but the value of trying to use the language even if one makes mistakes. The point is to see mistakes as steps towards better English, not as things to avoid at all costs.

Elementary Checklist

This could be translated into the students' own language.

Things to look out for in my homework	
1 I need to be careful with *he / she / it* + *'s'* in the present simple.	
2 I used present simple instead of past simple.	
3 I need to be careful with spelling.	
4 I need to make my sentences shorter / longer.	
5 I didn't use the definite article.	
6 I put in unnecessary articles.	
7 I need to make sure my verbs have a subject.	
8 I need to be careful of word order in questions.	

Intermediate Checklist

Things to look out for in my homework	
1 I need to use more linkers.	
2 I used the wrong linker or too many linkers.	
3 I need to be careful with spelling.	
4 I need to check any irregular past simple verbs.	
5 I left out the definite article.	
6 I put in unnecessary articles.	
7 I didn't use paragraphs.	
8 I used language that was too formal.	
9 I used language that was too informal.	
10 I didn't write a conclusion.	

Finish It At Home: 1

Level	Any
Aim	To make homework a cooperative activity; to provide support to the less able students
Duration	5–10 minutes in class, 30 minutes at home
Materials	None
Skills / Language	Varied

Procedure

1 Towards the end of the class, explain the homework task. For example:

You are going to write a story beginning with the words:
'He was the strangest man I had ever met ...'

2 Brainstorm ideas and language (vocabulary, connectors, tenses, etc.) and put them on the board.

3 Dictate the first words of the story to the class.

4 Ask the students to write the next sentence or two.

5 Ask them to compare each other's texts so far and add the next sentence to their texts.

6 Get feedback and check errors.

7 Ask them to finish the story for homework.

NOTE: This technique can be adopted for any genre of text: letters, discursive, argumentative, opinion, reports, and so on.

Finish It At Home: 2

Level	Any
Aim	To make homework a cooperative activity; to provide support to the less able students
Duration	15–20 minutes in class, 30 minutes at home
Materials	None
Skills / Language	Varied

Procedure

1 Dictate the first sentence of a story. For example:

A man was walking down the street.

2 Read out the following questions and ask the students to make notes of their answers.

What did he look like?
What was he wearing?
Where was he going?
Why was he going there?
Was he going to meet anyone?
How was he walking?
Was he alone?

3 Ask the students to compare notes and help each other with ideas.

4 Ask them to finish the story for homework.

Variation

Give less able students support by providing more questions, (e.g. about the background to the story):

What was the weather like?
Where does the story take place?
Who else was in the street?
What time of year was it?

Memory Tests

Level	Any
Aim	To learn new words and phrases
Duration	Variable at home, 10 minutes in class
Materials	A list of words or phrases learnt in class
Skills / Language	New vocabulary

Procedure

1 Hold a quick whole-class discussion on what the best way to remember new words is (with low levels you can do this in the students' own language).

2 Write up the suggestions on the board, incorporating some of your own. See suggestions in the box opposite.

3 Direct the students to the vocabulary (words or phrases) they have learnt in class recently. Choose between fifteen and twenty items.

4 Tell them to choose **one** of the memory methods and to use it at home to test themselves on the vocabulary.

5 In the next lesson, tell the students to take out a piece of blank paper and write down the words they remember with a translation or definition (depending on the level).

6 Tell them to compare with a partner. Who has remembered more? Which system works better?

7 Repeat these last three stages for the next lesson.

8 Go back to the original set of words two weeks later and ask them to write as many as they can remember.

Ways of Remembering New Vocabulary

Make a list with the translation next to it.

Make a diagram showing how the words relate to each other.

Draw pictures of the words.

Say the words out loud before you go to sleep and when you wake up.

Make a story with the words. Read the story to yourself two or three times.

Ask another person to test you on the words at home. Ask them to test you over and over again.

Repeat the words over and over again.

Write example sentences containing the words.

Make cue cards with the words on one side and a definition / translation on the other.

Put the words on cards with a definition on the back and test yourself while you are waiting in a queue.

Write the words on Post-it notes and put these around the house, in the car or on your diary.

Transform It

Level	Any
Aim	To revise classwork at home; to personalise grammar exercises
Duration	10–15 minutes in class, 15–30 minutes at home
Materials	A typical grammar / vocabulary exercise from the coursebook
Skills / Language	Sentence transformation

Procedure

1 Go through the grammar / vocabulary exercise in your usual way. The following example is from an intermediate-level exercise:

Nobody asked me for my opinion of the idea. (thought)
Nobody asked me _____ the idea.

This is the best music I've ever heard. (better)
I've _____ this.

She was the only one who didn't enjoy the film. (apart)
Everybody _____ her.

2 Make sure all the students have the correct answers to the grammar exercise.

3 At home, the students rewrite the original sentences from the coursebook to make them more personal, for example by adding the names of people they know to the original, impersonal sentences. They then transform them in the same way they did in class. They should come up with something like the following:

My parents didn't ask me for my opinion about our holiday this summer.
My parents didn't ask me what I thought about our holiday this summer.

Beethoven's symphonies are the best music I've ever heard.
I've never heard better music than Beethoven's symphonies.

Marialena was the only one who didn't enjoy the film.
Everyone apart from Marialena enjoyed the film.

Follow-up

For an exam-based version of this task, see In Reverse: 1 and In Reverse: 2 on pages 116 and 117.

Hometeach

Level	Any
Aim	To review the English students have learned by asking them to teach it
Duration	5 minutes in class, 20 minutes at home, 5 minutes in class
Materials	None
Skills / Language	Varied

Procedure

1 Tell the students that for homework they must find someone (at home, preferably) who has a lower level of English than they do and offer this person a free lesson. This could be their parents, siblings or partner.

2 At the end of the lesson, give the students five minutes to think about and plan their lesson. They can look at their coursebook or other lessons that they have done. Tell them they should exchange ideas on what to teach with other students (this will help those who don't have any ideas on what to do).

3 For homework, they have to give the lesson and then be prepared to report back.

4 In the next lesson, ask the students to report back to each other on their mini-lessons. Do some whole-class feedback on this. You can ask questions such as:

What did you teach?
Who was your 'student'?
How long did the lesson last?
Did you enjoy it?
How did your 'student' react?
What have you learnt about teaching: is it easy / difficult?

Variation

You can ask the students to prepare a short 'lesson' and then teach each other in class the following day. They can do this in groups.

Writing to Each Other

Level	Any
Aims	To give a purpose to students' writing
Duration	10 minutes in class, 1 hour at home
Materials	Pen and paper; copies of a letter or e-mail you have written to the class
Skills / Language	Varied

Preparation
Write a 'letter to the class' or an 'e-mail to the class'. See examples below.

Procedure
1 Give a copy of your 'letter to the class' to the students.

2 Give them your address and ask them to write a reply at home and post it, so you receive it at home.

3 Reply to any letters you receive. If you can afford it, post your replies along with the original letters. Alternatively, put them in an envelope and 'deliver' them in the next lesson.

4 The students read your reply to their letters and take note of useful expressions that will help their own letter-writing. Get them to focus on the layout and structure of the letter.

5 Put the students in pairs and get them to exchange addresses.

6 At home, they now write a letter to their partner. They post it. On receiving the letter, the student writes a reply and posts it.

7 In the next lesson, the students bring a copy of the two letters for you. You take them home and write a general letter to the class. In this letter, you provide feedback on the content and language of the letters **as a whole**. This final letter closes the cycle and acts as a summary of what has been learnt from the whole letter-writing process.

Variation
A similar task can be set up using e-mail, where students have e-mail. Copies of the e-mail messages should be printed out or 'cc-ed' to the teacher.

NOTE: This whole process is a classroom return on their investment for those students who wrote you a letter, and it will make those who haven't done the homework realise what they are missing!

Beginner-level Letter

> Dear class,
>
> My name is Lindsay Clandfield. I am your teacher for this year. I am from Toronto, Canada. I live in Spain with my wife, Sofia, and two children: Marcos and Lucas.
>
> Please write and tell me something about you. I look forward to hearing from you.
>
> Lindsay

Intermediate-level Letter

> Dear class,
>
> Hi. My name's Luke and I'm just dropping you a line to introduce myself and so I can start to get to know you a bit. I am from the UK but I've been living in Greece for quite a few years now. I've been married a long time and we have three kids: Rosa, Michael and Antony (the twins!).
>
> Why don't you drop me a line to tell me a few things about yourself and your family? I look forward to hearing from you.
>
> Luke

English in My Home: 1

Level	Any
Aims	To raise awareness of English outside the classroom
Duration	5 minutes in class, 20 minutes at home, 10 minutes in class next day
Materials	None
Skills / Language	Varied

NOTE: This activity works best in monolingual settings where English is not the native language of the country.

Procedure

1 Put the following table on the board and ask the students to copy it into their notebooks.

English In My Home			
Kitchen	**Living Room**	**Bedroom**	**Other**

2 For homework, ask the students to find any and all items they have in their house with English words on them. Tell them to write the English words they find at home in the relevant column on the list.

3 In the next lesson, ask the students to work in small groups and compare lists. Write the following questions on the board for them to discuss:
Who has the most English in their home?
Where do you find most English words?
What do the words mean?

4 Follow this up with a discussion on the presence of English in the students' country. What do people use English for? Why?

English in My Home: 2

Level	Any
Aim	To learn vocabulary of things around the students' homes
Duration	15 minutes in class, 20 minutes at home, 15 minutes two classes later
Materials	Post-it notes or paper and adhesive tape
Skills / Language	Varied

Procedure

1 Distribute Post-it notes (or slips of paper with adhesive tape) to the students and ask them to make a label for everything in the classroom that they can. The labels must be in English.

2 Tell the students to put the labels around the classroom in the correct place (it is best to check if they are correct before you do this).

3 At the end of the lesson, tell the students to choose a room in their home and to do the same.

4 Tell them to leave the labels there for two days.

5 After two days, tell them to remove the labels and bring them to class.

6 Put the students into groups of three or four. Tell them to show each other their labels and explain what the words are (if they can remember them!).

Variation

Instead of bringing in the labels, tell the students to ask a friend or family member they live with to rearrange all the labels so they are on the wrong things; they then have to try to label everything again correctly.

Acknowledgement: We learnt the Variation on this activity from Jim Scrivener.

English All Around You

Level	Any
Aim	To raise students' awareness of English as an international language; to expose students to authentic uses of English in their own environment
Duration	Variable at home, 15 minutes in class
Materials	None
Skills / Language	Varied

Preparation
Collect and bring to class some examples of 'real English' (e.g. supermarket products, advertisements in magazines).

Procedure
1 For homework, ask the students to keep a record, in a special notebook, of words and phrases found in the environment: graffiti on walls; the names of shops, clubs, and so on; the names of magazines (local and imported) and brand names.

2 In the lesson, instruct the students take it in turns to present their findings, which should be written on the board in categories and copied into their notebooks. For example:

Graffiti
No war!
All property is theft

Magazines
Status
Business
Focus

Shops, Pubs, Clubs
Relax
Blow Up
Corner
Fast Food

Brand Names
Pampers
Tasty
Softex

3 Once this pattern is established, make the presentation of findings into a guessing game. The first student reads out the examples of English and the other students have to guess the type: shop, pub, cereal, clothes, etc.

Phrasal Verb Hunt

Level	From intermediate onwards
Aim	To encourage students to notice specific language items in a natural context
Duration	20 minutes at home, 20 minutes in class next day
Materials	None
Skills / Language	Phrasal verbs

Procedure
1 For homework, ask the students to search for phrasal verbs in a natural context. They could look:
- on the Internet
- in their coursebook
- in an English novel from the library
- in the newspaper
- on the street (if they are in an English-speaking country).

2 Set a number of phrasal verbs to find (e.g. five). Explain that when they encounter a phrasal verb, they should record it along with the sentence and source they found it in. They could also use a dictionary to record what the phrasal verb means (or a translation).

3 In the next class, tell the students to share the phrasal verbs they have 'hunted' in small groups. Elicit examples from the groups to put on the board – make it a 'trophy room'.

Variations
You could ask students to find examples of phrasal verbs in different genres of text. For example:
- an advertisement
- a poem
- a story
- a news item
- an informal letter
- a note.

You could set this as homework **after** you've presented the language item, or as homework **before** you present it: that way you have some authentic examples to start off with.

You can do a 'hunt' for any structure (e.g. a verb form or tense) or lexical item (words in a lexical field, synonyms, idioms, etc.). We provided phrasal verbs as an example because understanding phrasal verbs is much easier if one encounters them in real life rather than in coursebooks.

Pictures in My House

Level	From elementary onwards
Aim	To practise the skill of describing pictures
Duration	50 minutes at home, 10 minutes in class
Materials	Copies of pictures (your own and ones students bring from home)
Skills / Language	Speaking; *there is / there are; in the background / foreground / in the middle of the picture*

Preparation
Choose and bring in a painting of your own choice which you will describe to the students. You can bring a copy of the painting to class or make an OHT copy of it.

Procedure
1 Describe your painting to the students.

2 Provide them with key words and expressions for describing pictures in English.

3 For homework, ask the students to choose a painting. It could be one hanging up somewhere in their house or a painting from a book or a magazine if they prefer. They should:
- describe the painting in note form
- say why they like it
- find out and write something about the painter
- bring the painting (or a digital photo of the painting) to class if possible.

4 In the next lesson, ask one of the students to come to the front and show their picture to the class. They use their notes to say a few words about the painting and why they like it.

5 The other students then ask a few questions about the painting and / or the painter, which the presenter tries to answer.

6 Repeat the last two stages in subsequent lessons, with different students bringing a picture to talk about.

Follow-up
The students give you a copy of their notes. This text has been used to guide their presentation to the rest of the class, but it can also be re-used as a gap-fill activity with the whole class. You simply use the notes to write out a continuous text with gaps which the students then give to the whole class as a kind of revision.

My Song

Level	Any
Aim	To integrate students' interests into the lesson
Duration	20 minutes at home, 5 minutes at home, 5 minutes in class
Materials	None
Skills / Language	Listening

Procedure
1 Tell the students that for homework they have to listen to a song in English. They must try to transcribe the words. Ask them to bring the words and a recording of the song to class.

2 Collect in the homework (words and song).

3 Choose one song and produce a complete / correct version of the text, by adding the parts the student failed to transcribe. If you can't make out the lyrics yourself, try to find them on the Internet.

4 Return the homework, including the complete version, to the student.

5 Ask the student to gap the text (making, for example, ten gaps) and return the gapped text to you.

6 Use this gapped text as a completion task for the whole class.

7 Get the students to check their answers by listening to the song.

Variations
Ask the students to write a resumé of their favourite lyrics (the original lyrics may be in English or in their own language): what is the song about?

Ask the students to:
- write a story built around the characters and situation referred to in the song
- write the biography of the main characters in the song
- write a translation of the song
- find out some facts about the singer / group on the Internet.

NOTE: Songs are a popular 'way into' English. You can make this a regular feature of your classes, asking for a different student's song each week.

Watch It!

Level	From elementary onwards
Aim	To integrate homework with real-world activity
Duration	1–2 hours at home
Materials	For students: DVD or video
Skills / Language	Listening; speaking; present simple (for narratives)

Preparation

Prepare a short synopsis of a film that you like:

> ### King Kong (2005)
> Set in the 1930s, this is the story of a group of explorers and documentary filmmakers who travel to the mysterious Skull Island to investigate legends of a giant gorilla named Kong. They discover that King Kong is a real creature who lives in a massive jungle with creatures from prehistoric times. The explorers search for the great ape, fighting Kong and his dinosaur enemies. Finally, King Kong is attracted to the beautiful human in the expedition. The explorers capture Kong and take him back to New York, where he is put on display, but of course he escapes and is free in New York.

For lower-level students, a model could be provided, like this:

> ### King Kong (2005)
> *Set in* (when and where), *this is the story of* (who or what). *It stars* (actors, actresses). *I thought it was* (adjective). *Some of the lines I can remember in English are* (insert memorable lines here):
>
> - ....
> - ....
> - ....

Procedure

1 Explain that the students must choose a DVD / video in English (with or without subtitles depending on the level).

2 Ask them to watch the film and jot down words or phrases that stand out or catch their attention. They should have about twenty such expressions by the end of the film.

3 Tell them that they will be expected to use these notes as a guide for telling their partner or group about the film.

4 In the next lesson, give your presentation of a film you saw and liked (the box opposite gives an example).

5 Put the students into pairs or groups of three and tell them to take turns describing their film to the others, using their prompts. Circulate and help.

Follow-up

The students write a review of the DVD / video.

Phone Survey

Level	From elementary onwards
Aim	To report on information found outside the classroom
Duration	Variable in class, 90 minutes at home
Materials	None
Skills / Language	Speaking

Procedure

1 Explain to the students that they are going to conduct a survey by telephone. They are to collect information about (a) people's opinions (b) people's habits and routines. Suitable topics for a phone survey might be:

Holidays
The most popular places

Sport
The most popular sports

Consumer habits
Where people shop and what they buy

Roles in the home
Who does which chores

2 Brainstorm the questions that will be needed for the investigation. Here is an example for 'Consumer Habits':

What have you bought in the last week?
(a) food
(b) clothes
(c) electrical equipment
(d) furniture

Where were these products made?
(a) in our country
(b) abroad

Were they … ?
(a) expensive
(b) cheap
(c) reasonably priced

Were you happy with the product?
(a) yes
(b) no

3 Put the students into groups to choose a topic for their survey.

4 The groups write their questions collaboratively in English, although they may have to ask them in their own language during the survey.

5 At home, the students phone friends and relatives and ask the questions in their survey. They take note of the answers.

6 In the next lesson, students sit with the others in their group and compare results.

Variations

The students produce a written report of their findings. For this variation, it is a good idea to spend some time first, explaining how the report should look (title, paragraphs, organisation of data).

The students produce posters of their results which are displayed on the walls.

In the News

Level	From elementary onwards
Aim	To link classroom work with real-world tasks
Duration	30 minutes at home, 15 minutes in class
Materials	A collection of headlines from the news
Skills / Language	Reading; speaking

Preparation

Collect seven or eight headlines from the current news to bring to class.

Procedure

1 At the end of the lesson, write the headlines on the board.

2 Ask the students to work in pairs and choose one headline.

3 Tell them that for homework they must find out more about this news item.

For higher levels:
Tell them to research the news item on the Internet, using an English news site (e.g. www.bbc.co.uk).

For lower levels:
Tell them to research the item using the Internet or newspapers in their own language.

4 In the next lesson, put the students into the same pairs and tell them to compare their findings. They must prepare a short (three-minute) presentation about this news item.

5 The students swap partners. Each student should be sitting with someone new.

6 Tell them to explain their news story in English to their partner.

NOTE: When the students have done this activity once, they can choose their own news stories for the next time.

Poster Project

Level	Any
Aim	To integrate language and skills and to link classroom work with real-world tasks
Duration	Variable in class and at home
Materials	At home the students will need a poster, pictures, coloured pens, glue
Skills / Language	Varied

Procedure

1 Go through your coursebook lesson in the usual way.

2 Choose a topic from the book as a basis for a 'poster project'. For example: *Sport Around the World*.

3 Explain the framework of the project:
- Find information about the most popular sports and sports stars in different countries.
- Take notes.
- Collect pictures.
- Stick photos and pictures on the poster.
- Add notes about the country, the sport and the sports personalities.
- Use different coloured pens.
- Make your poster eye-catching.

4 The students bring their posters to class.

5 Organise an exhibition and ask the students to stand next to their posters and answer questions, giving information about the topic of their poster project.

NOTE: If you provide the class with a number of possible projects to choose from, this not only provides more choice, but the exhibition phase will also be more interesting.

You can also put students into pairs so they can help each other and learn to work cooperatively.

Correcting Homework

Correction Questionnaire

It is important to know how the students themselves like to be corrected. To find out, what better way than to ask them?

- Elicit from the students the way they like to their oral and written work to be corrected.
- Add their ideas to your own in order to construct a 'Correction Questionnaire'.
- Prepare the questionnaire and hand it out.

How I like to be corrected – speaking

In spoken work, I like the teacher to:
- ☐ write my errors on the board
- ☐ use translation to correct me
- ☐ tell me: *no, that's wrong*
- ☐ echo what I say correctly
- ☐ finish what I want to say when I can't remember
- ☐ correct me immediately
- ☐ wait until I've finished speaking
- ☐ correct me later, when the activity is over
- ☐ make a tape of my errors and play it back
- ☐ ignore unimportant errors

How I like to be corrected – writing

In written work, I like the teacher to:
- ☐ correct all my errors
- ☐ correct only the more serious errors
- ☐ indicate the kind of error in the margin (e.g. prep = preposition; sp = spelling, etc.)
- ☐ indicate the location of the error only
- ☐ tick correct items, cross incorrect ones
- ☐ summarise the main errors at the end
- ☐ write comments in the margin
- ☐ write comments on the content
- ☐ read out errors and ask the class to correct
- ☐ dictate wrong sentences correctly

Allow students to complete the questionnaires and collect them in. In the next lesson, point out which were the most popular choices. Explain that you will use a variety of correction techniques from this list, including the most popular.

Constructive Correction

It is important, too, to stress certain strategies for raising the 'profile' of homework and giving it more value in the students' eyes than is often the case. For example:

- When you collect the students' homework to check it, add more personal comments on the work they've done. While a 'very good' is better than nothing, feedback becomes more meaningful if it is specific and can also reflect on earlier work and progress.
- Be consistent with marks and comments. If a piece of homework is not very good, or was done in a rush, then say so. It will make the other, better, comments and praise more worthy.
- If you have gold stars or other stickers, you can put them on good work along with comments. This practice doesn't have to be restricted to children. As the teacher Maria Tzovaras says, there is no student in the world (young and old, believe me) that does not find a small dose of joy in receiving a sticker for a job well done.

Above all, use 'errors' as a starting point or 'pretext' for further learning – recycling gives new life to what is usually thought of as useless.

Caring Criticism

Getting back a piece of homework with the same old comments tacked on at the end (*good, very good, try harder ...*) or with no comments at all is a disheartening experience and does little to motivate the student to do more homework or better homework. If you vary your comments on students' written work, it is not only more likely the students will read them, but they may actually be motivated to act on them! Here is a variety of ways of responding to students' written work:

Positive Comments
A lovely piece of work.
This was an excellent piece of work.
I especially like the way you ...
The (X) ... was especially good.
You've made a lot of progress in this area.
You're using the language we've learnt in class very well.

In-need-of-improvement Comments
I think you need to work on ...
There are very few mistakes in this homework, but the vocabulary / grammar is very simple. At your level I think you can use more complex structures / words.

Responding-to-the-content Comments
Is this a true story? Amazing.
What a frightening / funny / exciting experience.
What happened at the end?
I agree / disagree.

Writing and reading homework is a two-way process; we hope students will reciprocate the interest we show in their work. It is important not to underestimate the power of words to shape attitudes.

Homework RAP

Traditionally, reading and correcting homework is an opportunity to find out what students have or have not learnt and to make sure they get effective feedback on their errors. This remains fundamental to the purpose of correcting homework, but correction can also be an opportunity for achieving much more in terms of the students' approach to learning. We can have an impact not only on **what** students are learning but **how** they learn. These additional benefits of correction can be summed up in the acronym 'RAP': Rapport, Attitude, Participation.

Through the way we correct, we can build better rapport between teacher and students, we can build more positive attitudes towards learning and, ultimately, we can extend students' participation in the learning process. Here are some tips for creating 'RAP' in the classroom:

- Give the students opportunities:
  to check their own work
  to check each other's homework (but always monitor and provide feedback on such tasks to make sure they don't identify mistakes wrongly or reinforce mistaken ideas).
- Use a marking code such as the one below to activate the students' involvement in the correction process.

If the students can correct their own work, this tells you that the 'deviant' language was merely a slip or superficial mistake rather than a serious error.

Correcting Codes

Here is a sample code you might use to correct work:

^	=	something missing
#	=	number or agreement
WO	=	word order
WW	=	wrong word
VF	=	wrong verb form
WF	=	wrong form
T	=	tense
Prep	=	preposition
Art	=	article
?	=	what do you mean?
Sp	=	spelling
P	=	punctuation
Ø	=	not necessary
NA	=	not appropriate in this context
[	=	start a new paragraph

This is only a sample – each teacher will have their own preferred style of code. The important thing is to be consistent.

DIY Correction

There is a simple procedure for using a marking code like the one above with large classes, but first you must make sure the students learn it.

- Raise student awareness regarding the variety of correction processes: self-peer, group, teacher-group, teacher-student, teacher-class, etc.
- Teach your marking code.
- Work through the following steps:
  1 The students attempt to correct their own work.
  2 In pairs, they engage in peer-correction.
  3 The pairs join up to form groups.
  4 Monitor the groups, facilitating the correction process.
  5 'Tutor' individuals while the groups work alone.
  6 Do some teacher-class feedback.

Set aside time every week to go through this process. The group nature of the correction will help exert pressure on the students to do the homework!

Codes of Behaviour

While it is good to get the students to 'do it themselves' it is, first and foremost, up to us, the teachers, to take a positive and constructive attitude to homework correction and have our own code of good correcting behaviour. Here are some suggestions:

- Avoid using terms like *error* or *mistake* and prefer, instead, more positive terms such as *slips*, *attempts* and *good tries*.
- Approach errors and mistakes as evidence that learning is developing and, as such, as necessary steps in the learning process.
- Make a habit of correcting errors that affect the meaning of a whole sentence rather than correcting minor language points inside a word or phrase.
- Take a balanced approach between accuracy and fluency. If you insist on accuracy on all times then you will be forever trapped in correcting **all** deviant language.

And remember: don't use correction as a display of teacher power – let the students have the power ... and the glory!

Second-time-around Homework

Level	From intermediate onwards
Aim	To draft and edit a piece of written work
Duration	Variable
Materials	None
Skills / Language	Editing written work

Procedure

1 Next time you assign a piece of written work, collect it the following day and keep it for a week. Look at the work, but **don't mark it**.

2 When it is time to assign more writing homework, hand back the original written work, unmarked.

3 Tell the students that you want them to work on the same piece of writing, but to make it even better. Tell them that once they've done this, then you will give it a mark and comments.

4 Collect the writing homework the next day. Mark this second draft.

NOTE: Most students often won't bother drafting writing unless they are made to do it in class. This forces them to re-examine a piece of work and take the time to improve it.

Acknowledgement: This activity came from Paul Seligson at a workshop at TESOL Spain in 2004.

Second Draft, Third Draft

Level	From intermediate onwards
Aim	To develop writing skills through process writing
Duration	15 minutes in class, 1 hour at home
Materials	Pen and paper
Skills / Language	Drafting written work

Procedure

1 Give the students a topic to write about, For example: *How to Deal with Waste*

2 Brainstorm ideas and write them on the board for five minutes.

3 Tell the students to use the ideas on the board to write about the topic for ten minutes. They should write as fast as they can and produce as many words as they can (errors at this stage should be ignored). They can use note-form, too.

4 After ten minutes, stop the writing and ask the students to write a second draft at home, correcting as many errors as they can.

5 Ask the students to bring the second draft and a photocopy of the second draft to the next lesson.

6 In the next lesson, tell them to exchange the photocopies with a partner.

7 For homework, ask the students to write a third draft. They can use material from their partner's second draft (the photocopy) if they wish.

Follow-up

In the next lesson, collect in the drafts. From one of the students' pieces of work, produce a fourth draft, which can act as a model and for feedback with the whole class.

Recycling Homework

Level	From elementary onwards
Aim	To encourage students to do their homework
Duration	10–15 minutes in class
Materials	A 'Find Someone Who' questionnaire for each student (copied from the board or dictated to the class by the teacher)
Skills / Language	Speaking; focus on tenses

Procedure

1 Set the class some homework that involves extensive reading (to read a magazine article, a chapter from a book, etc.). Tell the students to write a few words by way of a summary of what they have read.

2 Collect in the homework.

3 Use the students' homework summaries to construct a questionnaire like the one below:

Find someone who:	Name
1 read an article about the *Titanic*. 2 read an article about rock music. 3 read an article from *Newsweek*. 4 is reading a book by Agatha Christie. 5 is reading a sports magazine. 6 has just finished *The Count of Monte Cristo*. 7 has just started a Sherlock Holmes story.	

Ask more *yes / no* and *wh-* questions to continue the discussion, for example:
What did you think of it?
Why did … ?
Have you read other articles about … ?

4 When you return the homework, give the students each a copy of the questionnaire.

5 Students circulate and ask and answer questions to complete the questionnaire.

6 Do some whole-class feedback, asking, for example:
Who can tell me someone who read an article about the Titanic?
What did they say about it?

Providing Models

Level	Any
Aim	To provide feedback on homework
Duration	10–15 minutes in class
Materials	A composition by one of your students
Skills / Language	Listening

Procedure

1 Collect in the students' compositions and correct them.

2 Choose one of the **worst** pieces of homework. If the text is long, take a continuous extract and make a correct version. If the text is short, you can do the whole text. Keep the student's original ideas, only correcting grammar, vocabulary and punctuation.

3 Without saying whose homework it is, explain that you are going to dictate one student's homework.

4 Dictate the correct version to the whole class.

5 The students compare their 'dictations' in the normal way.

NOTE: By choosing one of the worst pieces of homework, you are validating the student's effort and also (discreetly) showing them how it can be improved. Additionally, the 'worse' students are probably not accustomed to having their work held up as a model and it may encourage them to do better in the future.

Good Tries

Level	Any
Aim	To give feedback on homework
Duration	5–10 minutes
Materials	A list of correct and incorrect sentences from the class homework for each student
Skills / Language	Writing; editing and correcting

Preparation

Read the students' homework and select a dozen sentences (a mixture of correct and incorrect ones) to make a worksheet.

Procedure

1 Give each student a copy of the worksheet. Explain that these are all 'good tries' at the homework.

2 Tell them that some of the sentences are correct and some are incorrect (for weaker classes, you can tell them how many are correct).

3 Ask the students to work in pairs or groups to identify the correct sentences and correct the incorrect ones.

4 When they have finished, go through all the sentences with the class making sure that at the end everyone has twelve correct sentences on their worksheet.

Discussing Homework

Level	From elementary onwards
Aim	To focus attention on particular errors in homework and make it a supportive activity
Duration	15 minutes.
Materials	Written homework; a 'Find Someone Who' worksheet (see below)
Skills / Language	Speaking; a mixture of tenses and modal verbs

Peparation

Make a 'Find Someone Who' worksheet containing items that reflect the typical difficulties your students are having. For example:

Find someone who:	Name
1 needs to be careful with spelling.	
2 needs to use more linkers.	
3 used the wrong linker.	
4 should use linking sentences more.	
5 left out the definite article.	
6 put in an unnecessary article.	
7 mixed up the past simple and the present perfect.	
8 did not use enough paragraphs.	
9 used language that was too informal.	
10 did not write a conclusion.	

Procedure

1 Hand back the marked written homework and let the students read through the comments you have made. If you have done the activity Check After, Check Before on page 93, then let them complete their tables.

2 Distribute the 'Find Someone Who' worksheet.

3 Tell the students to stand up and circulate. They must ask questions to find names to go next to the sentences. Demonstrate by asking a student:
Did you use enough paragraphs?
Did you leave out the definite article?

4 Tell the students that they must have at least three different names on their list.

5 The students circulate, asking questions and filling in their sheet.

6 Ask them to keep the list of problems as a checklist for future reference.

NOTE: When the students repeat the task with different problem areas, they can identify things that are perennial difficulties for them and areas where improvement has taken place.

Playing Games

Level	Any
Aim	For students to self-correct errors from homework
Duration	20 minutes in class
Materials	None
Skills / Language	Varied

Preparation

Collect nine sentences with errors from the students' homework and make them into a multiple-choice exercise. For example:

Sample Errors
I keep fit by: joking / jogging.
A big problem today is: drugs / drunks.
I love my: uncle / ankle.
My father is: a beggar / a baker.
My father: beat me / bit me.
I eat when I am: angry / hungry.
There are two men and two women sitting on a: chauffeur / sofa.
My mother has problems with her: bag / back.

Procedure

1 Draw a 3 x 3 grid on the board and divide the class into two teams. Assign one team the O and one team the X.

2 Explain the rules:
- one team calls out a square that they would like to occupy
- you write the two choices on the board
- the team may consult and then must say which one is correct
- if they get the answer right, then they can put their 'mark' in the space
- if they get the answer wrong, it's the other team's turn.

3 The game continues like this until a team gets 'three-in-a-row'.

Variations

You can use errors from students' homework to make other games and competitions. For example:

The Race
Give out ten sentences from the homework (some correct, some incorrect). Which pair of students can find all the mistakes first?

Double Your Money
Read out sentences from the homework and allow the students to bet imaginary money on them. If the sentence is correct, they double their money. If it's incorrect, they lose it.

NOTE: The examples opposite are authentic 'oral' errors, collected during Luke's First Certificate interviewer experiences.

5

Teaching Exam Classes

'I'd like to do more fun activities in class, but I have to prepare them for the test.'

The main difficulty with teaching exam classes, or any class where exams have a role to play, is how to stop the exam from taking over everything we do as teachers. It is only too easy to abandon our usual teaching practices and to teach to the exam. This usually means practising the kind of test items typical of the particular exam our students have to take: gap-fill, multiple-choice, transformations, true / false, and so on.

Tests and exams were not designed to be taught in class on a regular basis: they are a way of checking the progress of our students and identifying problems to work on. Yet what we often find ourselves doing is test items **throughout** the year instead of developing the skills which are to be tested: speaking, reading, writing and listening. To make matters worse, we may be teaching towards a test which addresses language (grammar and vocabulary) without skills – which means that we prize grammar and vocabulary over everything else in the class and give few opportunities for speaking, one of the main reasons people learn a language.

5.1 Making the Most of It

'I'd love to drop the test, but the system insists on it.'

This first section provides a number of suggestions and principles for how to make the most of your exam classes. It addresses the question: *How can test items be used to bring out the best in the students?*

The table below summarises the approach we have taken, in contrast to the traditional 'testing' approach of many classrooms. Here 'testing' refers to a way of teaching which is influenced by a 'testing mentality', rather than what happens when students take a formal test.

Testing	Teaching
... is product-oriented	... is process-oriented
... is failure-oriented	... is success-oriented
... is stressful	... is relaxing
... is individualistic	... is group-oriented
... is competitive	... is collaborative
... works with one right answer	... accepts more than one answer
... withdraws support	... provides support
... is context-less	... is context-sensitive
... is culture-bound	... is culture-sensitive
... is monotonous	... is varied
... uses closed-ended exercises	... uses open-ended tasks
... is teacher-controlled	... allows learner-control
... is judgemental	... raises self-esteem
... measures success in marks	... measures success in many ways

5.2 Teaching Not Testing

'It's hard not to let the exam dominate everything, but I have to make sure my students are prepared.'

The second section of this chapter includes activities that will help you 'work exams' in a creative and learner-friendly way. Research into memory suggests that we remember things which are unusual, humorous or 'outstanding' in some way. Clearly, memory plays an important part in a three-hour exam during which the use of reference material and other learning resources is forbidden. The more the candidates remember, the better they will do in terms of scores. The use of humour and topics that relate to the students' experience and cultural background transforms the usual gap-fills and multiple-choice exercises where form is all important and content counts for little into more memorable learning.

5.3 Testing without Tears

'My students panic so much about the test they can't concentrate.'

The activities in the final part of this chapter are designed to help reduce the anxiety associated with tests (usually associated with marks and results). They are not designed to replace tests, but rather help you 'test without tears'.

Tests, as all teachers know, are also the simplest and quickest way to impose discipline on an unruly class. They are a form of extrinsic motivation. The sudden announcement of an impending test will calm the beast in learners and increase attention and attendance.

However, tests can also be a source of immense anxiety, anxiety which leads to the detriment of other classroom activities. The 'backwash' (or 'washback') effect is the direct or indirect influence of examinations on teaching methods. This effect may be negative or positive. The negative effect means that many methods of teaching English fail to be applied in the classroom because both teacher and students are trapped in an exam-preparation cycle that is difficult to escape from. From the students' perspective, negative backwash makes language learning a stressful textbook or testbook-bound process. In most learners, it raises anxiety levels and leads to inferior performance.

It goes without saying, however, that testing at the right time and in the right proportions has a valuable contribution to make in assessing learners' progress and proficiency. Some tests provide useful and even communicative activities for normal classroom use; but this 'positive backwash' is sadly the exception rather than the rule in most exams.

Exams are not going to go away. Any suggestions concerning the 'teacherfication' or 'learnerfication' of exam material must take this fact of educational life into account. Everything in this chapter has therefore been based on this reality and on exam material. It is not an **alternative** to exam material. We have tried to show how the most unpromising material might be transformed into a vehicle of curiosity and self-expression, without teachers having to abandon their examination syllabus.

Making the Most of It

Tortoises and Hares

In 'testing' rather than 'teaching' procedures, the quiet and often erroneously labelled 'slow' learner is often penalised by the collective assumption that a 'quick' answer is better than a 'slow' one. Thus, 'fast' students put their hands up and shout answers, filling the pause that is created by the quiet students while they ponder their answer.

- Provide learners with 'thinking time' and where necessary fill this time with helpful prompts and follow-up questions.
- Encourage the quiet or slow learner, choosing one of their essays, rewriting it and using it as a model for the whole class.

Testing abhors a vacuum. Teaching, on the other hand, fills these pauses with useful hints and prompts and thus helps not only the faster students to come up with a right answer or a partially right answer.

In and Out

It is important to use lead-ins and follow-ups when presenting a topic or even a simple comprehension question.

- Don't be satisfied with getting the correct answer from the best student in the shortest possible time.
- Provide an opening for the quieter students and increase their chances of participation.
- Draw on the students' own knowledge and thereby facilitate learning.
- Show that the topic being tested is not just a mechanical device for eliciting a correct answer.

Lead-ins arouse interest and get everyone involved and thinking. Follow-up comments and questions send out a positive signal to the class, telling them that the activity is of intrinsic interest.

Getting Personal

Encourage the students to respond to tests in a variety of ways, not just in terms of correct / incorrect. There are various ways of doing this.

- Ask for a personal response to a reading / listening text. For example:

What did you feel after you read the text. Why?
What kind of person do you think the writer is? Why?
Would you like to read more about the topic?
Do you agree / disagree with the writer?

- Ask for a personal response to the test experience. For example:

How did you feel about this test?
Do you think you could have done better? How?
How could the teacher help you better prepare for a test like this?
How could you help yourself better prepare for a test like this?

This way the test becomes an opportunity to develop better learning habits, better class routines and more skills practice.

Test Types

Part of being successful at language tests means being able to understand test question types, not just the language being tested.

- In answering gap-fill or multiple-choice type tests, students should make a habit of reading the whole text before choosing.
- In preparation for gap-fill tests, students should learn whole phrases rather than individual words: learning collocations is useful preparation for tests of grammar and vocabulary.
- When dealing with sentence-level test items, you should show interest in the content, relate the fragment to a real-world context; arouse and satisfy the students' natural curiosity about those shadowy nouns and pronouns on the page.

Whatever test type you use with your students, it is important to ensure that they get a chance to practise with the question type first. It's unfair, for example, to include a sentence transformation exercise in a test if the students have never encountered one before in class.

Correcting Tests in Class

Part of testing includes going through the answers. There are things that you as a teacher can do to make this a more positive learning process for the students.

- Don't stand close only to the 'good' students waiting for the right answer – this leaves out the rest of the class and is bad for group dynamics.
- Don't fix your gaze on the good students or only the 'bad' students; this gives the impression you are 'testing' them.

- Use eye contact to **include** rather than **exclude** as many students as you can. Don't look **only** at the student answering a question or volunteering information: cast an eye over the rest of the class to ensure they are paying attention and to send a signal that when one student is speaking 'we are all involved'. Otherwise, the eye contact can convey the message to the rest of the class that 'I am only interested in checking up on that individual student; the involvement of the rest of the class is not important'.
- Occasionally get students to read each other's work and even to evaluate it using the official criteria – avoid test answers becoming exclusively 'for your eyes only'.

Testing should ideally have 'positive backwash' – meaning that the test has a good effect on teaching and the learning environment.

Error or Terror?

Your students will take more risks if they feel safe when speaking out.

- Avoid creating error-phobia. Use errors as **positive** steps in learning.
- Don't be obsessed with correcting all errors immediately – this will make quiet students even quieter and make your better students even more dominant.
- Don't monopolise authority in exam-preparation classes; the premium placed on the 'one right answer' inevitably inflates teacher power; our role becomes that of the arbiter of success and the fount of wisdom.
- Use techniques and management processes that validate and value the students' contribution.

It is in testing situations that we become 'the expert' and, as a result, cramp the potential of the students. A learner-input approach is a good way to embark on this delegation of authority.

On Your Marks ...

Finally, we have seen that marks earned in tests can be very motivating but they can also demotivate those students who are not collecting enough of them.

- Use marks sparingly and judiciously and prioritise successful attempts at using language rather than complete formal success.

- Give verbal feedback rather than quantitative results.
- Avoid classifying the class into 'good, bad, worse, worst'. Some learning qualities are not easy to measure.
- Make testing a group activity with group results as an occasional alternative to the traditional 'lone ranger' approach to testing where the isolated student struggles alone in competition with other 'candidates'.
- Take every opportunity to make students feel they have achieved even a minor success.

Computer-corrected tests insist on 'only one right answer', which is a pedagogically limiting concept. So where possible, when checking test answers in class, you may find you can accept more than one answer and that the alternatives are often produced by those 'quiet' students you want to encourage.

Naming Names

Level	Any
Aim	To personalise test sentences; to empower students to produce their own test items
Duration	10 minutes
Materials	Multiple choice / gap-fill test items from the coursebook / testbook
Language / Skills	Varied

Procedure

1 Give the students multiple-choice or gap-fill sentences consisting of six or seven items. For example:

I suggest _____ her a box of chocolates for her birthday.

2 Ask them to rewrite the stem sentences replacing the **pronouns** with the names of people in the class or other people they know. They may use the names of famous people if they wish.

3 Tell them they can also change any **vocabulary items** to make the sentence refer to a 'real' situation or one imagined by the students. For example:

I suggest _____ Luke a new briefcase for his birthday.

4 The students exchange their rewritten sentences with other members of the class and complete the test item. They write the answers on a separate sheet, to allow the sentences to be done by more than one student.

5 Do whole-class feedback, during which students read out their completed sentences. Use some of the sentences for follow-up discussion.

Without Distractors

Level	Any
Aim	To give students insight into how exam questions are constructed
Duration	20 minutes
Materials	A reading comprehension test with multiple-choice questions
Language / Skills	Varied

Procedure

1 Write the questions (but not the distractors) of a comprehension test on the board.

2 Ask the students to open their books at the reading comprehension test and to cover the questions. They should look only at the text, not the questions (keeping them covered up if necessary).

3 They read the text and answer questions you have written on the board.

4 Ask them to uncover the multiple-choice questions and choose the correct option.

NOTE: A brief note on the use of distractors can be found at the end of Dual Choice, Multiple Choice on page 61.

Multiple Choice Minus One

Level	Any
Aim	To give students insight into how exam questions are constructed
Duration	20 minutes
Materials	A reading comprehension test with multiple-choice questions
Language / Skills	Varied

Preparation

Prepare a copy of a multiple-choice reading comprehension test, minus **one** distractor. For example:

> *What does the writer say about Sue's career?*
> **A** *She took a long time to become famous as a tennis star.*
> **B** *She is better known as a TV presenter than a tennis star.*
> **C** *She obtained a better TV job after a short time.*
> **D** _____.

Procedure

1 Ask the students to read the text and choose the correct option.

2 Ask them to add one more distractor themselves.

Variation

- Prepare a copy of a multiple-choice reading comprehension test without the questions. For example:
  > _____?
  > **A** *She took a long time to become famous as a tennis star.*
  > **B** *She is better known as a TV presenter than a tennis star.*
  > **C** *She obtained a better TV job after a short time.*
  > **D** *She has tried a career in pop music.*
- Give the students the text and answers to the reading comprehension.
- The students read the text and write the missing question:
  > *What does the writer say about Sue's career?*

Jumbling Distractors

Level	Any
Aim	To make multiple-choice a teaching rather than a testing device
Duration	10 minutes
Materials	Test items from the coursebook / testbook
Language / Skills	Varied

Procedure

1 Take six multiple-choice test items (sentence-level only) and write up the options, including the distractors, on the board, in random order. For example:

> fee   agree   fit   reward
> like   bribe   tip   suit

2 Ask the students to identify words with a similar form or meaning and to group them together.

> **Group 1:** agree, suit, like, fit
> **Group 2:** bribe, reward, fee, tip

3 Check any items of vocabulary the students may not be sure about.

4 Ask the students to choose between one and three items and to write example sentences of their own.

5 They now do the test in the book in the normal way and, at the same time, check their example sentences with the original test items.

> *Would it _____ you if we came on Thursday?*
> **A** agree   **B** suit   **C** like   **D** fit

> *The service was so good, we gave the waiter a large _____.*
> **A** bribe   **B** reward   **C** fee   **D** tip

Gender Bender

Level	Any
Aim	To encourage students to interact more with the meaning of test items
Duration	15 minutes
Materials	Sentence-level test items
Language / Skills	Varied

Procedure

1 Take any test of grammar or vocabulary that refers to male or females. An intermediate-level example could be:

Although he overslept, Clive wasn't late for work.
Harry couldn't get his parents' permission to buy a motorbike.
John's behaviour at the party annoyed me.
Sheila had to finish the accounts and write several letters as well.
Sally decided not to do her homework and went to a nightclub.
Diane was supposed to write to her parents last week.
My grandfather was sixty when he learnt to swim.
Liza's grandfather is teaching her Chinese.

2 Ask the students to rewrite the sentences, changing males to females and females to males. For example:

Although she overslept, Karen wasn't late for work.
Harriet couldn't get her parents' permission to buy a motorbike.
Joanna's behaviour at the party annoyed me.
Shawn had to finish the accounts and write several letters as well.
Luke's grandmother is teaching him Chinese.

3 Follow up this exercise by asking the students to decide which sentences have changed most. Are they all still correct / possible? Which ones sound strange? Why?

Follow-up

As a further option, you can ask the students to write a report on men and women in this exam:

Men tend to oversleep and go to work, they behave badly at parties and they learn to ride motorbikes and to swim when they are old. ...
Women do homework and go to nightclubs, they do the accounts and they write letters. But they also learn foreign languages, like Chinese ...

Further questions, using this task as a starting point, could also be:

Is this text true of male / females roles in your country?
What are the gender differences in different countries?

In Reverse: 1

Level	Any
Aim	To recycle test items in a different way
Duration	15 minutes
Materials	Gap-fills (sentence-level or text-level)
Language / Skills	Varied

Procedure

1 Give students a gap-fill type test. For example:

I'd _____ not spend another day at the beach.
You can change your view of life, _____ to psychologists.

2 After they have finished, go through the answers and ask the students to correct themselves.

3 Tell them to turn over the page and give them one of the missing words from the test. For example: *rather*

4 The students must try to remember the original sentence from the test that required the word and write it down:

I'd rather not spend another day at the beach.

5 Repeat the procedure with another word. For example:
according
You can change your view of life, according to psychologists.

6 When they have finished, tell them to check their answers with the original sentences or text.

Variation

You can adjust the level of difficulty of the reconstruction by providing the students with more or fewer words from the original gapped text:

I'd rather not

The students write:

I'd rather not spend another day at the beach.

In Reverse: 2

Level	From elementary onwards
Aim	To recycle test items in a different way
Duration	15 minutes in the first lesson, 15 minutes a week later
Materials	Sentence transformation tests
Language / Skills	Syntax; grammatical structures

Procedure

1 Give the students a series of transformation type test questions to practise a grammatical structure or element of syntax that you have been working on recently. For example:

> Jill cooks better than Bill.
> Bill _____.

2 After they have finished, go through the answers in the normal way.

3 Tell them to turn over or cover their questions. Now give them the answer sentences and tell them to transform them back again.

> Bill doesn't cook as well as Jill.
> Jill _____.

4 After a week or so, revise this test by repeating the above stage. Give the 'answers' and tell the students to transform them back into the original.

Beginning, Middle, End

Level	For intermediate onwards
Aim	To integrate grammar and writing tests; to make exam composition part of writing skills development
Duration	60 minutes at home
Materials	Sentence-level test items
Language / Skills	Varied

Preparation

Take any sentence or sentences from a sentence-level grammar test that you have already administered and write them on separate pieces of paper (some of the sentences can be repeated). For example:

> Elizabeth hadn't realised the film had started.
> (to practise: didn't know that)
> He no longer works at Sony.
> (to practise: no longer versus used to)
> The trip was cheaper than he had expected.
> (to practise: cheaper than versus not as expensive as)

Procedure

1 Distribute the test sentences. Ask the students to write a short composition and to include their sentence at the beginning, middle or end of their composition.

2 When the students have handed in their compositions, redistribute them to other students and ask them to find the original test sentence and write it down.

3 Do whole-class feedback to make sure everyone has a list of the sentences which have been re-used.

NOTE: Students are often asked to write a story beginning or ending with a particular sentence. For example:

> The telephone rang as she was leaving the house.
> It was the most important day of his life ...

Grammar or use of English tests that consist of random, context-less sentences make them poor vehicles for remembering what the student has to do in the examination. This activity makes the sentences found in grammar tests the basis for a narrative composition. It is a good way of recycling such sentences and making them more memorable. The technique has the added advantage of giving students a good reason for reading each other's compositions.

Variation

Give students more than one sentence to include in their compositions.

Lost Sentences

Level	From intermediate onwards
Aim	To make exam composition part of writing skills development
Duration	15 minutes
Materials	Composition titles from past papers
Language / Skills	Varied

Procedure

1 Dictate two or three composition titles from past papers:

   A *A meal when everything went wrong*
   B *The most popular tourist sites in your country*
   C *A letter of complaint to a tour operator after a disastrous holiday*

2 Ask the students to draw up a table with three columns: A, B and C (one column for each title).

A	B	C

3 Read out some sentences, one by one, and ask the students to write them in the correct column, like this:

A	B	C
The potatoes were still hard.	We have thousands of visits of every year.	The hotel was a two-star hotel not a four-star.

4 Ask the students to compare their answers and then check in whole-class feedback.

Follow-up

For homework, the students choose one of the essay titles and write their composition using the dictated sentences as well as their own ideas.

Your Sentences, My Essay

Level	From intermediate onwards
Aim	To make exam writing an interactive skill
Duration	60 minutes at home
Materials	Composition titles from past papers
Language / Skills	Varied

Procedure

1 Read out a number of narrative titles from past papers.

2 For each title, ask the students to write down the first and last sentence of their narrative composition on a piece of paper.

3 Tell the students to exchange their sentences with someone else.

4 They each write a story, ending with each other's first and last sentence.

5 When the composition is complete, the students read each other's compositions.

Variations

The same technique can be applied to other composition types (argumentative, letters, descriptive).

The exchange can take place at the note-taking stage: students write a composition using each other's notes. This will increase their awareness of the usefulness of note-taking before writing a composition.

Cut Them Up

Level	From intermediate upwards
Aim	To develop writing skills through topic sentences; to make exam reading interactive
Duration	10 minutes
Materials	Reading comprehension texts from the coursebook / testbook
Language / Skills	Varied; writing and reading

Preparation

Take the first sentence of each paragraph of a reading comprehension text and write them on slips of paper. There should be one sentence for every two students in the class (this may mean repeating sentences). For example:

Women who want to change their jobs cannot because they have the wrong qualifications.
Women can't find the opportunities they need.
It is difficult to convince girls that they should take up scientific subjects.

Procedure

1 Put the students into pairs. Give one sentence to each pair and get them to write notes on the topic in their sentence.

2 They compare their notes with another pair (or group) of students. They combine their notes to make two paragraphs for a composition.

3 Ask the students to write a composition for homework using these sentences.

4 When they have handed in their compositions, they do the reading comprehension test as it is in the book.

5 Ask the students to compare the original test with their own composition: what similarities and differences can they find?

Hidden Treasure

Level	From intermediate onwards
Aim	To make composition writing interactive and fun
Duration	60 minutes at home
Materials	Composition titles
Language / Skills	Varied

Procedure

1 Ask the students to write a composition in their usual way but, as they write their composition, to include in the text, at random points, words from their favourite song. For example:

> *Dear Sir or Madam,*
>   *I am writing to ask for more information about the Safari Holidays which I saw advertised in the Daily News. I see skies of blue.*
>   *First, I would like to ask which animals live in the Park. Trees of green. Secondly, I wondered whether the 'luxury hotel' you mention doesn't spoil the environment. I see them bloom for me and you.*
>   *The main reason I am writing is to ask whether you can arrange a Safari Holiday for a group of four. And I think to myself. We are interested in coming in the middle of July. What a wonderful world. We wouldn't mind flying but we are not sure whether your tours are by plane or helicopter. The colours of the rainbow look so pretty in the sky. Another thing which is not clear is the difference between the 'Night Drives' and the 'Overnight Trail'. They're also on the faces of the people going by.*
>   *Finally, we would like to know whether I see friends shaking hands a package tour saying how do you do is possible from Paris.*
>   *We look forward to hearing from you, they're really saying.*
>   *Yours sincerely,*
>   *I love you.*
>   *B G Moaner*

2 The students exchange compositions and read each other's work. As they do so, they underline the words from the song buried in the text.

Follow-up

Play one of the songs to the whole class, accompanied by listening tasks of your choice.

From Questions to Composition

Level	From intermediate onwards
Aim	To integrate reading and writing tests
Duration	15 minutes in class
Materials	Reading comprehension test (a narrative text)
Language / Skills	Varied

Procedure

1 Ask the students to turn to the question page of a reading comprehension test, made up of multiple-choice, true / false or *wh-* questions. Tell them **not** to read the accompanying text.

2 Explain that they must use the questions as clues to building up a story. They should read the questions and infer the context (*who, what, where, when, why, how,* etc.). For example:

Why does the writer ask the postman about his baby?

A He is interested in the baby.
B He wants to create a good impression.
C The postman is always polite to him.
D The postman enjoys a chat.

From this, the student might infer that the writer asked the postman about his baby to be polite or because they both like chatting.

3 The students continue in the same way with all the other questions.

4 They do the reading comprehension (which should now be of much greater interest to them – and it should be much easier to identify the correct answers).

Variation

Before doing step 4, ask the students to write a story based in their notes:

"Mary had just had a baby and when she found out the postman had also just become a father, she always asked 'How's the baby'? One day, ..."

Heads and Tails

Level	Any
Aim	To make exam reading part of reading skills development
Duration	10 minutes
Materials	Reading comprehension texts from the coursebook / testbook
Language / Skills	Varied

Procedure

1 Before the students read the text, ask them to make predictions about what they are going to read by using one of the following, which you write on the board:

- the first sentence of the text
- the last sentence of the text
- the first and last sentences of the text.

You can also suggest other options, writing whatever is necessary on the board:

- two or three sentences drawn at random from the text
- words chosen from the text which are connected with the topic of the text
- the multiple-choice or true / false questions that accompany the text
- various pre-questions related to the topic of the text (e.g. agree / disagree statements).

2 During the reading, the students check their predictions. Who was closest in their prediction?

Follow-up

After the test has been completed in its original form, ask the class to do further activities, such as:

- Narrative texts: continue the text by adding the next sentence or short paragraph
- Argumentative texts: underline points they agree / disagree with.

When, Where, Who?

Level	Any
Aim	To make exam reading part of reading skills development
Duration	10 minutes
Materials	Reading comprehension texts from the coursebook / testbook
Language / Skills	Varied

Procedure

1 Give the students a reading text from an exam question.

2 Ask them to read it first quickly. Set a time limit (e.g. four minutes).

3 Ask the students to work in pairs and briefly tell each other what they have understood about the text (they could do this in their own language if they want). Ask a pair to share their answers with the class.

4 Ask them to do one or more of the following, individually:
- underline all references to time
- underline all references to places
- underline all references to people
- put a circle round all reference items (the above, plus *he / she / it / they / these*) and link them to the things they refer to.

5 Tell them to compare their answers in pairs and then go through the answers with the whole class.

6 Give the exam questions based on the text.

Musical Test

Level	From intermediate onwards
Aim	To use a song as a basis for (a) open cloze practice (b) listening practice
Duration	15 minutes
Materials	A song, preferably slow
Language / Skills	Collocation; listening

Preparation

Prepare a gapped worksheet to go with a song and make copies for the students in the form of an open cloze test (this is similar to the Use of English gap-fill test used in Cambridge First Certificate exams). See the Notes below.

Procedure

1 Tell the students they are going to do a typical exam-type activity with a text.

2 Distribute copies of the gap-fill test and ask the students to complete the gaps with a suitable word. Do the first one with them as an example. Don't tell them where the text comes from.

3 When they have finished, tell them they are going to hear the text and must check their own answers.

4 Play the song and let them check the answers themselves. If they don't get them all the first time, you can play the song again (they will be only too happy!) or simply go through the answers with them in the usual way.

NOTES: The text of the song should look like an exam text (which will make the musical phase a pleasant surprise). In other words, make it into a paragraph. It is important that the gaps you make can only be filled by one word. Putting gaps for collocations, prepositions, auxiliary verbs or pronouns works well. If you are not sure, give your worksheet to another teacher to 'test the test'.

Songs by artists such as Elvis Presley, Johnny Cash and Bob Dylan are suitable for this kind of activity – they shouldn't be too fast and they work even better if there is a spoken interlude. For example, Elvis' *Are You Lonesome Tonight?* is particularly well-suited.

Co-evaluation

Level	From intermediate onwards
Aim	To encourage self-evaluation of students' written test
Duration	15 minutes
Materials	Any test items
Language / Skills	Varied; writing

Preparation

Prepare a copy of the marking criteria of the written exam your students are going to take. Here is a sample of the sort of criteria for a writing test administered by an international examination body:

> **High pass (18-20)** Ideas well developed, easily understood. Clearly addresses the issue. Good control of both complex and simple structures. Some localised errors do not interfere with comprehensibility. Vocabulary generally appropriate.
>
> **Pass (14-17)** Ideas easily understood, but might not be well-linked. Addresses the issue. Good control of basic structures and basic vocabulary.
>
> **Poor pass (10-13)** Ideas understood but sometimes communication breaks down. Not well-linked. Does not address topic. Some errors of structure which make communication difficult.
>
> **Fail (0-9)** Ideas incomprehensible due to serious errors; irrelevant to topic; a lot of errors which make understanding difficult. Poor organisation and linking. Negative effect on the reader.

Procedure

1 Give out the marking criteria to the class. Use the students' own language to explain any difficult concepts and use examples from actual compositions to make these concepts clear. Ask the students to complete the writing test bearing these in mind.

2 When they have finished, the students mark their own work using the criteria and hand it in to you.

3 When going through the students' work, give it a mark using the same criteria.

4 Take the two scores (the student's and yours) and calculate the average between the two (student score + your score /2). This is the final score.

5 For feedback, you can initiate a diagnostic discussion in class, or between yourself and the students concerned, of any discrepancy between the scores.

Group Test

Level	Any
Aim	To experiment with a different kind of test; to encourage student cooperation in test preparation
Duration	20 minutes in class, 20 minutes after the test
Materials	Any test material
Language / Skills	Varied

Procedure

1 Put the class into test groups of four or five students. The groups can be heterogeneous in terms of ability. Make a note of who is in which group.

2 Give the class an outline of what is to be tested in the next test. The groups then do their preparation together. You may want to give them some ideas on how they can do this. For example:
- choosing difficult areas and reviewing them
- explaining things to each other
- testing each other.

3 Monitor the groups from a distance. Don't let yourself get drawn in to one group. If you do provide support, make sure it's minimal and evenly spread among the groups. Ideally this is work they do together.

4 On the day of the test the students take the test individually. Collect the tests.

5 Put the tests into groups (see step 1). Mark each test in the group and then calculate the average mark of the group's tests.

6 The next day, give each group their mark. Don't give individual marks.

Acknowledgement: Thanks to Mario Rinvolucri for this idea.

Cheat Notes

Level	Any
Aim	To reduce the stress of a test situation
Duration	Variable
Materials	None
Language / Skills	Varied

Procedure

1 Next time you announce a test, explain that each student will be allowed to bring to class one sheet of notes which they can refer to during the test.

2 Tell the students what areas the test will cover (e.g. units 4, 5 and 6 of the coursebook). The students can prepare their notes at home.

3 Before you administer the test, tell them to take out their page of 'cheat notes'.

4 Set the test. The students can refer to the notes **if they wish**.

5 Collect the tests and mark them in the usual way.

NOTE: When we have tried this activity we have noticed three things:

- It didn't make a noticeable difference to the final results (meaning that those who would have failed the test, fail anyway).
- The students said they felt more comfortable about the test (the notes provided security).
- Many students said they didn't refer to the notes at all during the test, as the mere fact of writing them out had committed most of it to memory.

This coincides with our own experience of taking tests as students: we often didn't have to refer to the cheat notes we had written as we already knew them.

The Joker

Level	Any
Aim	To reduce the stress of a test situation
Duration	Variable
Materials	Joker cards or slips of paper for each student
Language / Skills	Varied

Preparation

Prepare small slips of paper or cards with the word *Joker*, or a related image, one for each student.

Procedure

1 Before the test, explain that each student will be given a card with a Joker on it. Explain that Jokers are special answer cards.

2 Give the following rules.

- During the test, the student may exchange the Joker for one answer from the teacher.
- To do this, they must raise their hand and wait for the teacher to come to them.
- When the teacher reaches their desk, they must indicate which item they need help on.
- If the teacher gives them the answer to that question, they must return their Joker card and they can no longer ask for any answers.

3 Administer the test in the usual way.

NOTE: This works well with tests which have lots of discrete items in them. 'Giving' one answer makes a small difference in terms of the overall result but it can make a **big** difference in how the student feels.

Variation

You can make the Jokers cumulative – that is, if the student doesn't use the Joker in one test, they can keep it for the next (and therefore have two Jokers). We have found this works particularly well with younger learners, who end up **not** asking for help at all, so as to keep all their Jokers!

6

Professional Development

*'I rush from one lesson to the next and I hardly ever get the chance
to talk to other teachers. It's a lonely job.'*

Up until now, we have been discussing difficulties as if the only two parts of the equation were you and your students. But no teacher is an island, and the difficulties we mention in this book are shared by hundreds, if not thousands, of teachers.

We can learn to develop our classroom presence by reflecting on our own experience as teachers and, by becoming aware of our strengths and weaknesses, perhaps learn to build on the former.

We can also learn from those teachers who seem to have relatively greater success with classes than other teachers. Here is what a teacher with a reputation for 'presence' said about discipline in her class:

I had to get their attention in the way I spoke, what I said, the way I moved and so on. The last thing I wanted was to be seen as just another boring old teacher. The thing was to create an atmosphere which said we're having a good time together ... I didn't claim to be perfect. If I didn't know the answer to any of their questions, I'd admit it.
(Teacher in a private language school)

Research into teacher morale has shown that teachers working in supportive environments are far less likely to burn out. If you are finding it difficult to cope with your students, it might be time to start looking **outside** the classroom for help. Remember: you are not alone!

6.1 You Are Not Alone

We make some suggestions on how you can deal with difficulties collaboratively: from the simplest to the more elaborate, from the immediate solution for a particular problem to the wider issues within your own teaching environment.

6.2 Read On!

It is a pity to miss out on what others have thought about the problems you may be experiencing. Reading lessens our feeling of being alone and also begins to build the knowledge on which new skills can be built. So don't try to reinvent the wheel and, of course, don't believe that reading alone will solve all the problems. However, taking an interest in the subject, its theory, practice and development, is itself a form of teacher development. Books like the ones listed (and more!) may just help you to see things from a different angle and make a fresh start. In the end, this interest in your work shines through and communicates itself to students as enthusiasm, which research has shown is a prime factor in successful teaching.

Finally, reading about our teaching problems and the interesting research that has been done into these problems may even inspire us to engage in our own classroom-based research. This is an excellent way of growing more confident, more professional and more enthusiastic – which in the long run are the best remedies for many of the difficulties we face in class.

The long-term solution – if there is one – to the difficulties explored in this book lies in your hands, in your mind and in your own experience. This short chapter is about building up your confidence and skills in collaboration with others in a similar situation and taking responsibility for your own development.

This book's recommendations are finished but your further development may be just beginning. When he was in his 80s, the great Spanish painter Goya said 'I am still learning'. Perhaps we teachers can learn from great artists and, by making learning and development a life-long process, we can perhaps make our teaching just a little bit like a work of art.

You Are Not Alone

Discuss the Problem in the Staffroom

One of the best places to start dealing with difficulties outside the classroom is the staffroom. Between classes or at the beginning of the day is a good time.

- Ask other teachers informally how they deal with different problems.
- Share techniques that have worked with your colleagues.
- Listen to and be supportive of your colleagues, too.

It is crucial to avoid the downward spiral into endlessly complaining about students – sadly all too common in staffrooms.

Arrange a Teacher Meeting

If you do find you are not alone in having trouble with a class or an aspect of teaching (large classes, homework never getting done, etc.), a less informal exchange may be called for.

- Organise a teacher meeting to discuss it more formally.
- Draw up a new code of behaviour to be established in the school, or a set of suggestions on how to manage the problem.

It is always best if you have the support and participation of management for this kind of initiative.

Set Up a Workshop

Apart from encouraging teachers to get together for discussion, you can also:

- organise a workshop to address a particular difficulty
- invite an outside teacher trainer or speaker to deliver the workshop
- lead the workshop yourself.

The outcome of a workshop should be a practical activity (or activities) that teachers can go and try out in their classes 'tomorrow' or 'on Monday morning'.

Set Up a Swap Shop

An alternative idea is a 'swap shop', where everybody brings ideas relating to a certain theme (e.g. 'more speaking in English' or 'judicious use of L1') and presents them to the group.

- Bring up some ideas yourself to begin with to get things started.

- Have the group appoint someone to take notes and to write up the main points of the meeting. This role, of course, should be rotated.

The very fact of sharing makes the process of developing as a teacher less judgemental and threatening. The more teachers can be involved in this exchange, the more democratic it is and the less 'competitive'. 'Star teachers' are replaced by good members of a team, who note that outstanding teaching practice depends on the work done by others.

Organise a Teacher Development Group

All of the ideas mentioned so far can be brought together and synthesised over a longer period of time by the formation of a Teacher Development Group. The aim of such a group is decidedly not to 'train' teachers and assess their abilities but to create a sharing, supportive context in which teachers can grow together. Here are some ideas to get you started:

- Set up a teacher development group with the established aim of discussing and sharing teaching techniques.
- Try to find a regular time and place to hold a get-together.
- Focus on a different area each time.
- Set the first theme yourself and do some background reading (see Read On! on page 127 at the end of this chapter) to get things started.
- Find an article from a professional magazine or journal and distribute it a few days before the meeting.
- Discuss articles and issues brought up by the group in the light of what you have read and / or your own experience.

The atmosphere and ethos of such a group is, by definition, non-judgmental and exploratory.

Ask a Colleague to Watch You Teach

If you have been having trouble with a particular class, try asking a colleague you trust and respect to come and watch you teach (assuming, of course, this is possible, time-wise).

- Tell your colleague what you would like them to look out for (e.g. opportunities to have students speak, transitions between activities, moments when 'disruption' or lack of attention occur).
- Ask your colleague to make notes but **not** to interrupt the class.
- Find some time to share views and ideas about the class when it is over.

For most teachers, being observed is one of the most nerve-wracking experiences we have to go through. This is a great pity as it is also one of the best ways of discovering what kind of teacher we are: it helps get away from the 'lone ranger' view of teaching. Knowing ourselves is difficult without the fresh view an outside observer brings and it is an excellent way of 'not feeling alone'.

Watch a Colleague Teach

Do you have a colleague who is renowned for excellent classroom management or discipline? Have you always wondered how they do it? You'll learn a lot from seeing another teacher in action – and it is something that teachers don't get to do that often.

- Ask to sit in on their class once.
- Conduct an informal interview, before and after, and listen to how that teacher explains his or her success.

But we don't have to limit ourselves to 'good' teachers. It is often said that observing a bad lesson can teach us as much as observing a good lesson. This is a bit like saying 'I didn't like the film but it made me appreciate the films I do like'.

- Get away from the idea that we watch other people at work, whether teachers or not, in order to judge them.
- Change the framework and mind-set of observation to something like 'I am observing in order to understand the mechanics of teaching, in all its rich and subtle variety; how one thing we do in class has an impact on another'.

In observing other teachers, we are learning to see more clearly what teaching is all about.

Exchange Classes

Assuming always that this is possible, why not exchange classes one day with a colleague who is teaching at the same time as you? This tactic may also be useful in moments of stress with a particular class – it gives both sides a chance to calm down and reflect – and even appreciate the strong points of the other side.

- Get together after the class and compare notes. How did the classes go?
- Make suggestions for each other.

Suddenly having to face another group of students is another potentially refreshing process and a way of improving the way we see both teachers **and** learners.

Get the Management on Your Side

This may seem obvious, but you should be aware of school-wide behaviour policies.

- Talk to the Head Teacher or Director of Studies about what options are available to you.
- Ask them to observe a difficult class of yours (it is better if **you** initiate this, rather than them coming in uninvited) and talk about the problems afterwards.
- Suggest a review of behaviour policies if the current ones aren't working.

Behaviour policies developed in conjunction with all parties (management, teachers, students and parents) tend to be much more effective.

Get the Parents on Your Side

If you are working with younger learners, you should never underestimate the power of parents to help you deal with difficulties. Most parents want their child to do well at school but perhaps don't know how they can help.

- Keep communication lines open with parents through meetings, letters or phone calls home.
- Send **positive** feedback as well as **negative** feedback and explain why you are using the methods you choose.
- Invite parents to observe a class and discuss it with you afterwards.

Having supportive parents on your side can help immensely; at least, getting them 'on side' if not always on your side!

Get the School on Your Side

Some difficulties may stem from a negative 'vibe' in the school. It is difficult to analyse, but we all know the feeling when the 'norm' in the school has become alienation and cynicism – and when that cloud has descended over the school even positive things get interpreted through a negative filter. Here is a short list of things that we can do as individual teachers to help try and build a good 'whole-school ethos'. Some of them may involve convincing management.

- Suggest and start extra-curricular activities (like an English Club, or English Video Afternoon).
- Promote cooperation between departments (a joint wall poster project between the English department and another department).
- Encourage students to take 'ownership' of space by displaying their work (on classroom walls, in the halls, in the playground).

With such reciprocal involvement, you may see that the cloud that some teachers seem to carry with them like a sad aura has begun to fade.

Read On!

Appel J *Diary of a Language Teacher* Macmillan, 1995
A teacher's reflections on teaching in difficult state-school circumstances. You are not alone!

Campbell C and Kryswevzka H *Learner-Based Teaching* OUP, 1992
Recipes for using student-generated material in the classroom. Useful where there are few or inappropriate materials.

Cook G *Language Play Language Learning* OUP, 2000
One of the more theoretical books in this list, it offers an excellent rationale for many classroom activities that fell out of favour because they weren't 'meaningful' (e.g. drills, language games).

Cowley S *Getting the Buggers to Behave* Continuum, 2001
Although more for the British school system than the ELT classroom, it still contains lots of useful advice and interesting studies. Does what it says on the cover.

Cross D *Large Classes in Action* Prentice Hall, 1995
Lots of recipes for dealing with large classes, focusing on grammar activities and skills. There is a 'teacher's diary' after the activities to encourage critical reflection on the recipes.

Deller S *Lessons from the Learner* Pilgrims-Longman, 1990
Abundant humanistic activities for using what the learners' bring to class, literally and metaphorically, as a basis for teaching and learning.

Deller S and Rinvolucri M *Using the Mother Tongue* DELTA Publishing, 2002
Full of activities and a strong rationale on making the most of the students' mother tongue while teaching English. If you've been anti-L1 in the past (or work at a school that doesn't allow it), read it.

Dõrnyei Z *Motivational Strategies in the Language Classroom* CUP, 2001
A balanced combination of theory and practical advice with lots of examples from the author's own experience of dealing with demotivated students. An entertaining and well-researched handbook.

Dõrnyei Z and Murphey T *Group Dynamics in the Language Classroom* CUP, 2003
A very accessible introduction to the theory of group dynamics and its relevance to the language classroom.

Edge J *Cooperative Development* Longman, 1992
Practical activities for raising teachers' awareness of their role and potential, especially when working together in a supportive atmosphere with other teachers.

Hadfield J *Classroom Dynamics* OUP, 1992
Recipes on how to handle difficult classes in terms of management skills and motivation, within a humanistic, interpersonal and reflective framework.

Hess N *Teaching Large Multi-Level Classes* CUP 2001
Lots of activities and ideas for these kinds of classes, in recipe format.

Ioannou-Georgiou S and Pavlou P *Assessing Young Learners* OUP, 2003
An award-winning resource book on testing and assessing young learners. Offers a broad range of activities on assessment – both realistic and accessible.

Lantolf J and Thorne S *Sociocultural Theory and the Genesis of Second Language Development* OUP, 2006
A comprehensive but dense introduction to the work of Vygotsky, cooperative learning and its applications to ELT. Well worth the effort.

May P *Exam Classes* OUP, 1996
A useful recipe book on teaching rather than testing exam classes.

McManus M *Troublesome Behaviour in the Classroom* (2nd edition) Routledge, 1995
An analysis of discipline problems in general secondary education with lots of ideas that can help ELT practitioners.

Neill S and Caswell C *Body Language for Competent Teachers* Routledge, 1993
Looks at the effects of teachers' body language on classroom management. Also gives hints on how to detect trouble from students' body language. Great drawings.

Palmer P J *The Courage to Teach* Jossey-Bass, 1998
An inspiring and honest account of the many roles of the teacher and how they grow in difficult circumstances. The author's basic answer to discipline and motivation problems is to teach yourself, in both senses of the phrase.

Parrot M *Tasks for Language Teachers* CUP, 1993
A practical resource book for training and development. Deep and detailed, but good to dip into, especially in teacher groups.

Painter L *Homework* OUP, 2003
A whole book devoted to making homework less of a chore for teachers and learners. Great stuff!

Rinvolucri M *Humanising Your Coursebook* DELTA Publishing, 2002
Here you'll find some real gems of activities that are tried, tested and true. And it's compatible with your coursebook!

Rogers B *The Language of Discipline* Northcote House, 1994
Written by an expert in discipline in secondary education, it is essential reading for ELT practitioners.

Scrivener J *Learning Teaching* Macmillan, 2005
A detailed and imaginative approach to teacher development; with thorough analysis and inspiring ideas. This new edition is considerably longer, with good additions.

Thornbury S *How To Teach Grammar* Longman, 1999
Thornbury S *How To Teach Vocabulary* Longman, 2002
Two of the best books in the Longman 'How To' series, in our opinion. Offer just the right mix of theory and practice.

Underwood M *Effective Class Management* Longman, 1987
A beginners' guide to the basics of handling a class and the classroom.

Vygotsky L S *Mind in Society* Harvard University Press, 1978
A dense but essential analysis of the roots of cooperative learning, based on the authors' socio-cultural approach to language.

IATEFL *Teacher Development* The Teacher Development SIG Newsletter

professional
perspectives

professional perspectives is a series of practical methodology books
designed to provide teachers of English with fresh insights,
innovative ideas and original classroom materials.

Other titles in the series include:

Creating Conversation in Class
by Chris Sion
More than 100 imaginative ideas and stimulating
activities designed to get students talking in class

Humanising your Coursebook
by Mario Rinvolucri
A wide range of activities designed to extend typical
coursebook language practice by engaging students
creatively and productively

The MINIMAX Teacher
by Jon Taylor
Practical, easy-to-use activities that generate the
maximum student output from the minimum teacher
input

Using the Mother Tongue
by Sheelagh Deller and Mario Rinvolucri
Ready-to-use activities which make creative use of
the students' mother tongue in the language learning
classroom

The *Resourceful* English Teacher
by Jonathan Chandler and Mark Stone
A complete teaching companion containing 200
classroom activities for use in a wide range of
teaching situations

Talking Business in Class
by Chris Sion
More than 50 engaging activities to provide free-stage
conversation in professional classes

Unlocking Self-expression through NLP
by Judith Baker and Mario Rinvolucri
Over 100 integrated activities which draw on the
insights into communication provided by
Neuro-Linguistic Programming

Spontaneous Speaking
by David Heathfield
A series of drama activities which promote positive
classroom dynamics, build confidence and lead to
improved fluency

Challenging Children
By Henk van Oort
Over 100 imaginative and adaptable activities which
challenge young learners and make learning fun.

For a full list and further details of titles
in the *professional perspectives* series,
contact the publishers at:

DELTA PUBLISHING
Quince Cottage
Hoe Lane
Peaslake
Surrey GU5 9SW

Tel +44 (0)1306 731770
E-mail info@deltapublishing.co.uk
Web www.deltapublishing.co.uk